"Honest, disturbing, convi
not in statistics and theor
women in ministry and the judicatory structures they serve in this
Church. As a bishop in this church, I will suggest this compelling
account to all of our parishioners, especially adult faith formation
groups, councils, and call committees."

—**Bishop Tim Smith**, NC Synod, ELCA

"*Holy Mischief* tells truths both difficult and painful even as it cele-
brates the persistent strength of ministry and leadership of women
as pastors. This book highlights the voices of ordained Lutheran
women in the American south, whose ministry powerfully and
poignantly grounds the daily work of the church, but whose ability
to carry such power and poignancy is undermined and questioned
at every turn—even by well-meaning allies. Yet Makant does not
leave the reader to despair. Rather she shines a hope-filled light
on the story—a light that she challenges the church to make more
effulgent over the next fifty years."

—**Rev. Dr. Katherine A. Shaner**, Lutheran Pastor (ELCA) and Associate Professor of New Testament, Wake Forest University School of Divinity

# Holy Mischief

# Holy Mischief

In Honor and Celebration of
Women in Ministry

Mindy Makant

CASCADE *Books* · Eugene, Oregon

HOLY MISCHIEF
In Honor and Celebration of Women in Ministry

Cascade Books
An Imprint of Wipf and Stock Publishers
199 W. 8th Ave., Suite 3
Eugene, OR 97401

www.wipfandstock.com

PAPERBACK ISBN: 978-1-5326-4922-6
HARDCOVER ISBN: 978-1-5326-4923-3
EBOOK ISBN: 978-1-5326-4924-0

*Cataloguing-in-Publication data:*

Names: Makant, Mindy, 1969–, author.

Title: Holy mischief : in honor and celebration of women in ministry /
Mindy Makant.

Description: Eugene, OR: Cascade Books, 2019. | Includes bibliographi-
cal references.

Identifiers: ISBN 978-1-5326-4922-6 (paperback). | ISBN 978-1-5326-
4923-3 (hardcover). | ISBN 978-1-5326-4924-0 (ebook).

Subjects: LCSH: Women clergy—United States. | Women in church
work—United States. | Ordination of women—United States. | Women
in Christianity. | Sex role—Religious aspects—Christianity.

Classification: BV676 M255 2019 (print). | BV676 (ebook).

Manufactured in the U.S.A.                              09/12/19

Dedicated to the many courageous and grace-filled women accused of mischief-making who welcomed me into their lives and shared their stories with me.

# Contents

# 1

# "The Church Needs All of Us"

## Introduction

During the final months of interviewing for this project I was facilitating a workshop for female clergy. One of the pastors commented, "I only work at 75 percent. It is exhausting, this tap-dance of holding back so that I don't challenge or threaten my male colleagues. I mean, I'm pretty awesome at 75 percent, but can you imagine what I could do if I was free to be 100 percent me?" I asked the group whether or not others felt the same way. About half said they did. So I asked them how they held back, in what ways. One woman who serves as associate pastor with an older male senior pastor said she has to hold back to "manage the senior pastor's ego." Most of the pastors serving as associates agreed. I asked for specific examples, and another woman said, "I have to hold back from anything that might be perceived as unfeminine, so I hold back from exercising authority, I hold back from using power." Again, heads around the room nodded. A brief moment of silence, broken by a woman wistfully saying, "Just think what we could do if we were free to fully use our gifts rather than having to check ourselves to keep from threatening the men around us." Yes, indeed, just think where the church could be if all were encouraged to embrace their God-given gifts and use them for the sake of the gospel rather than holding back for fear of what others will think, say, or do in response.

Sheryl Sandberg makes clear in *Lean In: Women, Work, and the Will to Lead*, this (perceived?) need to hold back is not limited to women in ministry. Sandberg explores the sociocultural norms and expectations and the ways these expectations are internalized, which lead women to hold back. At the risk of blaming the victim (a risk she acknowledges) Sandberg puts forth this premise: it is at least in part up to women to change these norms. And the way women are to do this is to "lean in" by expecting to excel in their fields, to be taken seriously as leaders, and to change the dominant culture.[1]

For women in positions of ecclesial leadership all of the gendered norms are further complicated by layers of ecclesial traditions and particular hermeneutical lenses employed in Scripture interpretation. Sandberg's admonition to lean in is thus even more crucial for women in ministry—for their sake, but also for the sake of the church and for the sake of the world God so loves. But in a field where "success" is wispy at best and where faithfulness is the objective—as opposed to, say, a corner office—Sandberg's admonition to lean in begs the question, into what shall we lean?

One pastor I interviewed said that she hoped that the day would come when women would no longer be received as a consolation prize. This hope is not a placid, passive one, but something that this particular female pastor has spent decades working for. In fact, every single woman I interviewed for this project is actively working—some quietly, some loudly—towards exactly this goal. Together they are leaning into the hope that one day their voices will be heard as on par with those of their male colleagues; together they are leaning into the hope that one day the gifts of women in ministry will be valued as equal to those of men in ministry precisely because they offer a different perspective.

## Fiftieth-Anniversary History

In August 1970 the Lutheran Church in America (LCA) and the ALC (American Lutheran Church), the predecessor bodies of the current Evangelical Lutheran Church in America (ELCA), both approved the ordination of women. And on November 22 that

---

1. Sandburg, *Lean In.*

same year Elizabeth Platz became the first woman ordained in a Lutheran community (the LCA) in the United States. A month later, Barbara Andrews was ordained in the ALC. It took a few years—nearly a decade in some synods—for women to be ordained across what would become the ELCA.[2] And many female clergy, even nearly fifty years later, are still the only women in their conferences and the first female pastors members of their congregations have ever seen.

As women entered more fully into the pastoral leadership of the church, it took more than twenty years for a woman to be called to the office of bishop. April Larson was elected as bishop of the La Crosse Area Synod in 1992, where she served for sixteen years. In 2001 the first woman of color, Margarita Martinez, a Latina, was elected bishop of the Caribbean Synod. And in 2013 Bishop Elizabeth Eaton was elected as the first female presiding bishop of the ELCA.

In 2018 the ELCA elected six new bishops. It was a historic election; all six newly elected bishops are female, including the first two African American female bishops who were elected within twenty-four hours of each other. Patricia Davenport was named bishop in the Southeastern Pennsylvania Synod and then Viviane Thomas-Breitfeld was elected bishop of the South-Central Synod of Wisconsin. Also in 2018 Sue Briner (Southwest Texas Synod) was elected as the first female bishop to serve in the geographical region of this study.

As of this writing, approximately 35 percent of active ELCA clergy in the US are female. And roughly 50 percent of ELCA

2. The ELCA is divided into sixty-five geographic regions called synods. The word *synod* comes for the Greek for "walking together." Each synod has its own bishop and the ELCA as a whole has one presiding bishop. Synods, especially synods that encompass larger geographical areas, are often sub-divided into conferences or clusters of congregations. The conferences have deans (in some synods the deans are appointed by the bishop and in some synods they are elected by the conference pastors) who function in a largely administrative manner as an extension of the bishop's office. And area conference pastors often come together for pericope study (a study of the lectionary texts) and special worship services and they often work together to provide confirmation, Vacation Bible School, and youth group activities.

seminary students are female, And yet women in collars still confuse and anger people. That the ELCA and a number of other religious communities now ordain women illustrates a change in the hearts and minds of many (particularly in regard to scriptural interpretation)—otherwise a change in practice would not have been possible—but a change in practice cannot simply manufacture a change in the hearts and minds of those who oppose women's church leadership and ordination. Furthermore, many continue to resist women in ministry in practice even when they are supportive in principle. A number of the pastors I interviewed, especially those who have been in ministry thirty years or more, expressed feeling that the momentum toward the full acceptance of female pastors has been a one-step-forward, two-steps-back experience. Most of the clergy shared a sense of frustration, impatience, and even bafflement that a pastor's gender was still a conversation piece: "It amazes me that people can struggle so much with packaging." And yet all of the women I spoke with were determined to persist faithfully in their calling: "I don't want to change my gender. I want to be who I am, who I am called to be. But I wish it didn't have to be so hard sometimes." And all the women shared a sense of hope and expectation that the day would come when this conversation would cease to make sense. But that day is not today.

As we approach the fiftieth anniversary of women's ordination in the ELCA's predecessor bodies, this book leans into the hope that in another fifty years these conversations will be nothing more than a bewildering, if quaint, reminder of the way things used to be. At the same time this book is written in the belief that hope for a different—better—future is made possible by an imagination that is shaped by the past.

## Methodology

This project stems from my interest in intersections. I am fascinated by the intersection of culture and religious practices; of geography and social location, especially gender; of power and public performances of power; and of history, scriptural interpretation, and lived theology. In the spring of 2014 I read Colin Woodard's *American Nations: A History of the Eleven Rival Regional Cultures of North America*.[3] Woodard tells the story of the development of the United States not as a united cultural body but as distinct sociopolitical regions with different—often contrasting and sometimes conflicting—cultural expectations, social mores, and notions of the good. These cultural differences are rooted in concrete historical practices that, in many cases, have spanned several centuries with only minor adaptations. The eleven nations Woodard refers to are not clearly demarcated. That is, there is no clear boundary at which one ends and another begins. Rather, they are best understood as overlapping spheres of influence with many geographic locations simultaneously influenced by two (or sometimes even three) different cultural nations. The two "nations" Woodard calls the Deep South and Greater Appalachia are the regions that remain socially and culturally the most resistant to women in positions of authority, particularly spiritual authority. This resistance is rooted in a number of historical practices, including (but not limited to) modes of scriptural interpretation and notions of right authority, ecclesial and otherwise.

I am neither a historian nor a cultural anthropologist, so I cannot vouch for the veracity of Woodard's arguments. But as a theologian and an ethicist, and as a woman raised at the intersection of the cultures Woodard calls Greater Appalachia and the Deep South, I resonated with much of what he said. So, for reasons that are both practical (I live and work in North Carolina) and cultural (Woodard's Greater Appalachia and Deep South correspond roughly with the synods located in the South), I have focused this study on the experiences of female ELCA clergy living and serving in positions of public ministry throughout the American South: from Washington, DC, to Virginia to North and South Carolina to Tennessee, Georgia, Alabama, Mississippi, Louisiana, and Texas.

The bulk of the research for this project has been individual interviews. I have interviewed eighty-five female clergy. I have also interviewed every bishop (nine total) within the scope of the

3. Woodard, *American Nations*.

project as well as every ordained female assistant to the bishop who was serving at the time I interviewed the synod bishop.[4] The research for this project has been an absolute joy. Many, many things have surprised me, but the greatest surprise—by far—has been the opportunity to get to know so many incredibly gracious and loving people. Christ's church is in good hands. Hands that are caring and passionate, hands that are kind and tender, hands that are faithful and that ache for justice.

My approach has been to contact each of the ELCA's synodical bishops with jurisdiction in the research area, explain the project to them, and request a one-hour interview. Each bishop has been incredibly gracious with his time and supportive of the project. (And they have all been 'hims'; the first 'her' was elected during the final stages of this project and had already been interviewed as an assistant to the bishop.) After I interviewed the bishop, I requested interviews with any female clergy members of the bishops' staffs (assistants to the bishop or directors of evangelical mission[5]). I then asked each bishop and each bishop's staff member for the names and contact information for ten to fifteen female clergy within the synod whom they would recommend I interview. I have contacted many—not all—of these clergy and requested ninety-minute interviews with them. Not only were most willing, but many expressed excitement that someone was interested in their stories. A few were reticent, even when I assured them of anonymity. Even when I assured them that nothing they said would be reported back to their bishops. When I interviewed those whose names had been given to me by the bishops' staffs I

---

4. In the ELCA assistants to the bishop—in some synods referred to as associates to the bishop—are (generally speaking) pastors or deacons who accept a call to serve with the bishop. The specifics of their ministry as assistants to the bishop vary widely from synod to synod and from individual to individual. However, all of the assistants to the bishop serve as a judicatory leader as a representative of the office of the bishop within their synod.

5. Directors of evangelical mission are rostered ELCA leaders (generally pastors) who serve on behalf of the ELCA within each synod. They provide leadership within the synod relating to areas of mission and vision planning, congregational renewal, and stewardship.

then asked them who else *they* would recommend I interview. So, my list of potential interviewees quickly grew exponentially. And as the pastors I interviewed spoke to other female pastors in their own clergy support circles, I had clergy contact me *asking* to be included in the interviews. My only regret in my research is that I was unable to interview everyone!

The interview questions themselves are very open-ended. I have asked each pastor to talk about:

- their call story
- their experiences with candidacy and seminary, including responses from family and friends
- the most fulfilling aspects of public ministry
- the most challenging aspects of public ministry
- any advice they might have for women considering a call to public ministry

Whereas I did, many times, ask someone to say a bit more about something they alluded to, I avoided asking any specific questions. For example, in chapter 5 I talk about the number of female pastors who have experienced physical and sexual violence in ministry. I did *not* ask questions about experiences of violence; stories of violence came out, however, surprisingly often when women were asked what was most challenging about doing ministry. It is crucial that these stories came out unbidden; I strongly suspect that had women been specifically asked about experiences of violence or intimidation, the number would have been considerably higher than were reported during my interviews.

Similarly, I asked bishops very open-ended questions about their perceptions of what ministry was like for women in their synods. I did not ask, for example, questions about pay inequity or discrimination in the call process—though nearly every bishop mentioned these problems to me. I also asked bishops how they imagined this project might be helpful to them. I was touched by the sincerity with which the bishops answered this question and a bit overwhelmed by the sense that they want to know how to help the women in their synods, but they are at a genuine loss for what to do. Chapter 6 is my response to the bishops' requests for guidance on how to help the female pastors and candidates under their care. I offer it in hopes that this project will help the church live more faithfully as we move into the next fifty years of women and men serving in ordained ministry together.

Here is one methodological note about interview protocol and language: All the interviews took place between June 2016 and February 2019. In order to ensure anonymity, although no stories I've shared are manufactured, some are composites of similar stories, and the geographical details of nearly all of the stories are intentionally vague. No identifying information—including the dates of any specific interviews—is given, as even dates could identify pastors who work in a staff setting (e.g., pastors who work in the bishop's office or with a senior pastor). For ease and consistency I refer to all the parish pastors I interviewed simply as pastors. When referring to a bishop, I call the bishop a judicatory official if what matters is the administrative perspective, but I use the title bishop when it that role is crucial. For the assistants to the bishops who are also female clergy, I use whichever designation (*pastor* or *judicatory official*) is most appropriate to the story they are sharing.

A final note on polity: This project focused exclusively on female clergy rostered in the Evangelical Lutheran Church in America (ELCA) and serving either on synod staff or in a parish in the American South. The ELCA's polity structure includes synods (which are geographical), bishops (who have judicatory authority over both clergy and congregations within a synod), and a presiding bishop (who is the ELCA's head of communion)—a setup that may be unfamiliar or even foreign to members of other church bodies. My hope is that though the particularities of the ELCA and its polity may play an important role in understanding the nature of this study, the experiences of the clergy are not limited to women serving in public ministry within the ELCA but will resonate with clergy throughout the church. Where necessary I have tried to explain ELCA-specific language and practices in footnotes in that hope that readers from other denominations will be able to translate this into their own ecclesial language. Likewise, while I realize that a geographic focus on the American South necessarily shapes this study, my hunch is that many of the challenges that female clergy in the South face explicitly may be more subtle—but just as real—in other regions of the country.

And finally, here a few statistics: I interviewed a total of eighty-five female pastors (some of whom were serving as parish pastor at the time of the interview, and some as assistant to the bishop or as director of evangelical mission within their synods) and nine (male) bishops. Between the eighty-five female pastors there was—at the time of the interviews—a combined 1,340 years of experience in pastoral ministry. Thus the mean years of experience was 15.76, with the actual amount of experience for a given individual ranging from a few weeks to thirty-eight years. The majority of the female pastors were married. Eighteen were half of a clergy couple, but of those eighteen, five were married to pastors in non-ELCA traditions. Thirteen of the pastors interviewed were divorced, two widowed. Only one of the pastors interviewed identified as a member of the LGBTQ community. And—in my opinion the biggest demographic weakness of this study, but a fair reflection of the ELCA—only six are nonwhite.

Anne Lamott says that stories are like flashlights that shine a light in one place.[6] This book is intended to tell a story. Though it is not a single story, I have tried to tell it in as coherent a narrative form as is possible, and I hope that it illumines a particular place in our church. I have asked the women I have interviewed what they most hoped would come from their participation in such a project. And, as if with a single voice they have responded, "I just want my bishop and my male colleagues to *know*." To know how different it is to serve the church in a female body. To know how much more difficult even the most daily of tasks can be. They want their parishioners to know how much they love them, and how desperately they hope to serve them, and how much harder both parishioners and community members make it for female pastors to do their

---

6. Lamott, *Almost Everything,* 77.

jobs. And they want and need the whole church to know what they are doing for our sake, for Christ's sake, every day.

And yet head knowledge is not sufficient. We all know that women and men experience ministry differently, that men and women are received differently in the church. Ample studies and statistical data support this.[7] But data does not change hearts and minds. In fact ample studies show also exactly that—that we are rarely swayed to change our beliefs or practices by the sharing of data. However, sharing stories creates bonds and builds empathy. Learning another's story allows me to develop a level of imaginative empathy. We can never truly walk in another's shoes. However, the more deeply I can enter into another's story, the more likely I am to see the other as familiar and thus to want to advocate on her behalf. My hope is that in sharing the stories of women who are serving the Lord as ministers of Word and Sacrament within the ELCA as we celebrate the fiftieth anniversary of women's ordination in our predecessor bodies, the church will become more genuinely open to the gifts of women in ministry for the sake of the church, for the sake of the world, and for the sake of the gospel.

## Interview with ELCA Presiding Bishop Elizabeth Eaton

In the winter of 2017 I interviewed Bishop Eaton as a part of this project. Though her parish ministry has never been within the geographical purview of this study, it seemed critical to me to include the experiences and insights of the ELCA's first female presiding bishop. And as presiding bishop, she is in public ministry in the South. Bishop Eaton was a delight to interview, and she agreed to allow her interview to be published as is and without the anonymity granted all other interviewees. The transcript of her interview is below—my questions are in italics; Bishop Eaton's responses follow.[8]

7. See Fiedler, ed., *Breaking*; and Knoll and Bolin, *She Preached the Word*.
8. Makant, Eaton interview.

*Can you offer something of a bird's-eye view of the state of women in the ELCA? What do you see from your office?*

The "state" of women in the ELCA is not uniform. It is harder in certain regions—the South and Texas, for example—and it is certainly *much* harder everywhere for women of color.

It is probably most difficult for young, single women. Women are more often called to smaller, rural congregations, and thus find themselves in remote locations. I suppose this may be hard for young, single men too, but it does seem like a lot more young single women find themselves in this position, probably because young men will have many more options than young women will.

And, one of problems in these rural areas is that female clergy—and their parishioners—are more likely to hear "She's the devil" from non-Lutheran clergy in the community. And even by their own parishioners they are often seen as somehow or other less pastors than the male pastors (regardless of denomination) in the community.

This is especially a problem for women who have gone through the TEEM process.[9] Women seem to make up a disproportionately large percentage of TEEM candidates, and when they are ordained they are seen—often by other ELCA clergy—as "pretend" pastors.

And yet, with a growing clergy shortage, we need pastors. And women are often the ones willing to fill in the gaps.

*What do you see as the greatest struggles faced by female clergy?*

People will leave a congregation when/if it calls a woman. Every time. Every call I served had folks leave. Most of the time before they even met me. So, I learned not to take it personally, but it's hard. Because I know they left because I'm a woman.

---

9. TEEM (Theological Education for Emerging Ministries) is a certificate program that leads to ordained ministry within the ELCA without the requirements of residential seminary attendance. It focuses primarily in providing pastoral leadership to and in underserved communities.

And there are still congregations that will not even consider a woman. (Of course, many of these congregation also refuse to consider a person of color or someone who is gay or whose first language isn't English.)

I think for women appearance is much more of an issue than it is for men. People—men and women—feel like it is okay to comment on clothing, makeup, hair styles, etc. You are criticized for being too feminine and for not being feminine enough. It's like there is always the question—do you look like clergy? And yet our cultural image of clergy is still a man. So, female clergy have to try to "look" like a professional, like a pastor—which in people's minds is still often someone in a man's suit—without trying to look like an "imitation man." A lot of female clergy have started trying to accessorize more with their clerical collars, to try to find this line. But it takes an awful lot of mental and psychic energy to always be worried about how you're being perceived just because you're a woman.

Another problem is that some men—especially straight, white men—seem to be worried about the "feminization" of the church. This seems to be especially true of men who feel like the church has been the one—maybe the only—place left in our society where their authority has been assumed, unquestioned. And now more and more pastors are women. And the church is yet one more place where straight, white men aren't at the center.

One example—I love sports. I always have. I grew up with brothers and I know how to "talk" sports. Often this has given me an entree into conversations with men. But once I had a male parishioner tell me, "I don't like jockstrap women."

Another unique problem women face is problems with pregnancy and child care. Call committees interviewing young female clergy often ask, 'But what if she gets pregnant?!' Yet those same call committees don't ever think to ask, of a middle-aged male clergy, 'But what if he has a heart attack?!'

And some congregations—a lot of congregations—still treat maternity leave like sick leave. We are getting better as a church at granting both maternity and paternity leave, but it is very uneven.

*What impact, if any, do you think the ELCA's '09 deci-
sion on same-gendered relationships has on women in
ministry?*

I do think there is a connection between some of the struggles female clergy continue to have and the hoopla surrounding
the '09 decision. But I'm not sure what it is. It's odd. Like there is
something wrong, something sexualized by our embodiment, and
that if a woman is preaching or presiding over the Eucharist people
are focused on her anatomy. And if a gay person is doing it, they're
thinking about what he's doing in bed. It's nuts. No one does that
with straight male pastors.

I really don't think the fallout of the '09 decision is about
scriptural authority, or even about scriptural interpretation. It is a
more visceral response than reasoned one. It is more like a concern
about a system of belief becoming unraveled. If that's not true (appropriate gender roles), maybe the resurrection isn't true either. It's
a huge leap. But it's also more about what we often *think* is in the
Bible rather than what is actually in the Bible. ELCA Lutherans are
not the most biblically literate. I'm not sure we do so well at biblical
instruction much past a third-grade level.

*What unique contributions to the larger church do you see
women in ministry making?*

There are a lot of great women who are doing great ministry. And a lot of great men doing great ministry. And though I'm
sure there are gendered differences in how we approach ministry,
it's hard to know what is a result of gender and what is someone's
unique contribution.

As synod bishop I know there was a time, after a really messy
sexual misconduct, when I came in as bishop and someone commented that perhaps it was helpful to have a woman to really hear
what was going on. But this was a really messy case. Like most
sexual misconduct cases, the pastor was a charismatic man who
had done a lot of good—the church had really grown during his
tenure—but he was also a lone-ranger type and met with men from

his congregation in a town 'Gentlemen's Club.' And this group of men all covered for one another, they were having affairs.

*Would you share a little bit of your own story?*

I grew up in a faithful, Lutheran family. My father was a Sunday school teacher and my mother on the altar guild.

When I was in junior high school—the year *before* the decision was made to allow for women's ordination—we had to write an essay on what we wanted to be when we grew up. I wrote that I was going to be a Lutheran pastor. I don't remember having really thought about it before then. And the teacher told me I couldn't because the church didn't ordain women. But it was okay, because I also wanted to be music teacher and an actor and . . .

Later, my father's health problems triggered a series of theodicy questions—you know, why are these things happening to him, kinds of questions. My home pastor was very responsive. He gave me a good space for thinking through the questions. He didn't give me answers, just space for the questions.

The first example of a female pastor I had was in college. She was Presbyterian and she invited a group of college students to her house regularly for theological and spiritual conversation. We called ourselves the "heretic group." Again, she didn't really give us a lot of answers, but she gave me a space to ask questions. And to wrestle with a sense of call. So, when I graduated I decided to give seminary a shot. My parents weren't opposed to it, but they were worried because they knew there would be social problems. They convinced me not to go to a Lutheran seminary—to try something different. So I went to Harvard. My experience there was both totally disruptive and really, really helpful. After my first year in seminary I decided to go talk with my bishop. I did this backwards, but he was very supportive. And I began the candidacy process.

*How about your call to the Bishop's Office?*

I was someone who always said that we have to be ready to go where God is calling us. So, when I was elected as synod bishop in 2006, I couldn't really pull my name out even though I had no intention of running. I did want us to have a conversation about racism and homosexuality in the church. And since I wasn't trying to get elected, I went ahead and just said what I thought about this, about us as a church needing to be talking about these things. I guess folks wanted to talk about it more.

And of course the 2008 recession hit not long after that. And my synod was really hit by it, especially with the auto industry. And then there was the 2009 decision. One member of the synod lamented to me, "And now the church does this . . . ?!" There was so much uncertainty.

And yet, when I left the church I was serving to become a synod bishop I was followed by a male pastor. A child in the congregation remarked, "But, he's a boy!" So, things are changing.

*And your call to the office of the presiding bishop?*

I've always been a religious, not spiritual, person. But I began working with a spiritual director while I was a synod bishop. And when folks started saying I might be the next presiding bishop I contemplated pulling my name, not letting myself be available to be elected. I said this to my spiritual director, who asked me, "How do you know better than the Holy Spirit?" So, again, I decided to say the things I thought needed to be said. We [ELCA Lutherans] were becoming generic American Protestants and this was not helping us proclaim the gospel. We need to be the church, not another NGO. And, again, I guess people wanted to be talking about these things. More than I expected.

I know I'm the first female presiding bishop and sometimes I can't tell if people hear me as the first female presiding bishop or as the presiding bishop. I have tried to downplay the "first female" part—to say I'm the presiding bishop and I happen to inhabit a female body—but I have had so many people—men and women—who have said how grateful they are to be in a church that can call a female presiding bishop. And when I've presided over communion and served communion to someone with tears in her eyes because she never imagined such a day . . .

And I've been pleasantly surprised by the respect I've received. Especially in our Roman Catholic Ecumenical dialogues. Even with the Vatican. I am *always* referred to as "Bishop" and I no longer need a Roman Catholic (male) bishop to be with me to receive a salute from the Swiss Guard. Which is really cool.

*Any advice you'd like to offer?*

Sure, to women in ministry or exploring a call to the ministry—be yourself. Don't try to be or do ministry like a man. God calls men and women. And we all have gifts and struggles. This shouldn't be as hard as we sometimes make it. The church needs all of us.

## Suggested Resources

Evangelical Lutheran Church in America. *Faith, Sexism, and Justice: A Lutheran Call to Action*. Chicago: Evangelical Lutheran Church in America, 2019.

Evangelical Lutheran Church in America, North Carolina Synod. *Seriously? A Video of Actual Things Said to Women Pastors by Parishioners and Male Pastors*. Published October 10, 2018. https://www.youtube.com/watch?v=bTcaAkG86QQ&t=163s/.

———. "*Seriously?* Group Discussion Guide." Published October 2018. https://nclutheran.org/wp-content/uploads/2018/10/Seriously-Discussion-Guide.pdf/.

———. *Seriously?* Podcast series. 8 episodes. http://nclutheransynod.libsyn.com/.

Fiedler, Maureen E., ed. *Breaking through the Stained Glass Ceiling: Women Religious Leaders in Their Own Words*. New York: Seabury, 2010.

Sandberg, Sheryl. *Lean In: Women, Work, and the Will to Lead*. New York: Knopf, 2013.

Thompsett, Fredrica Harris, ed. *Looking Forward, Looking Backward: Forty Years of Women's Ordination*. New York: Morehouse, 2014.

Woodard, Colin. *American Nations: A History of the Eleven Rival Regional Cultures of North America*. New York: Penguin, 2011.

## Discussion Questions

1. What does it look like for you to "lean in" to your calling?

2. What is your first memory of a female religious leader?

3. What is the history of women's leadership in your own congregational or professional setting?

4. How do you think geography effects our experiences of gender? Race? Social class?

5. Bishop Eaton says we make this harder than it needs to be. What do you think about this?

# 2

# Wilderness Voices

The star of Pixar's 2017 film *Coco* is Miguel, a young Mexican boy with a passion and obvious talent for music. Unfortunately, Miguel's great-great-grandfather, a musician, abandoned his family when Miguel's great-grandmother was a toddler. As a result (and after much misplaced blame), Miguel's family adamantly opposes music and music making. The older he becomes, the more determined Miguel is to follow his calling to make music, and the more desperately his family attempts to silence his voice. When Miguel finds himself trapped in the underworld on the Day of the Dead, he discovers many truths about his family and—consequently—about himself. During a climactic moment in the film, Miguel's great-great-grandfather blesses Miguel, telling him, "One cannot deny who one is meant to be. And you, my great-great-grandson, are meant to be a musician." This blessing names Miguel and gives him a calling. Or, rather, it gives Miguel permission to follow the calling that he had known was there for many years but which had been forbidden to him. Furthermore, this blessing allows Miguel to find his voice.[1]

## Hearing Voices

Much like Miguel, many—though by no means all—of the pastors I interviewed found their voices silenced as they faced significant resistance while exploring the possibility that God had called

1. Unkrich and Molina, dirs. *Coco*.

them into public ministry. Quite a few of these pastors grew up in traditions other than Lutheran; for most becoming Lutheran was an integral part of the discernment into the ministry. A solid handful of the interviewees grew up in a congregation of the Southern Baptist Convention.[2] Many of the women interviewed said they had been very religious as children and always been attracted to church life.

One of the women who grew up Baptist said that she always "wanted to do something important in the church" and because becoming a pastor was an unthinkable thought, she dreamed about being a missionary or a pastor's wife—dreams that were encouraged by her family and church—from the time she was in kindergarten.

Another pastor who had grown up in a Baptist congregation said that even though she had always loved her church, she had also always argued with it. When she was five years old her Sunday school teacher told her mom to tell her to stop asking questions. When she was ten and asking the pastor questions about anything and everything. "I was arguing with him really," she says. He snapped at her one day, "I'm the pastor. What I say, God says. Don't question me." Such experiences with pastors, teachers, and parents, though often more subtle, are not uncommon.

One of the women I interviewed did not, as an adult, set out to be a pastor. She attended a Southern Baptist Convention seminary to be trained for youth ministry. The Baptist congregation of her childhood was supportive and encouraging. "Yet," she said, "in seminary I could not shake the growing sense that I was called to public ministry on a larger, congregational level." She told her home pastor and members of the deacon board this. They told her that she must have misunderstood the call of God. She found this to be terribly disorienting. These were they very people who had taught her to take God's claim on her seriously, and now that she was doing so they wanted to dismiss what she

---

2. I did not, as a rule, ask what tradition pastors grew up in. Eight of the eighty-five pastors told me they grew up SBC because it was an important part of their call story. It is quite possible that the actual percentage is actually higher and equally possible that this is a reality for ELCA pastors in the South that does *not* translate into other regions of the country.

was increasingly certain was God's voice. Despite the sense of betrayal, her remarkably bold response to the church leadership was, "I've not misunderstood God; perhaps you have misunderstood what it means to be faithful."

Women who grew up Lutheran often struggled with a lack of role models and support for following God's leading into full-time public ministry as well. Several of the women I interviewed grew up in pre-1970 ELCA predecessor bodies. One says she wasn't really discouraged from thinking about ministry; her father was a pastor and encouraged her questions, and though he never told her she could be a pastor, he never tried to dissuade her either. But he didn't have to. The church would: "I realized I was called to be a pastor. And I *wanted* to be a pastor. But we weren't ordaining women yet. So I slowly gave up on that dream and did the things that society expected of me. Years later when I was well into adulthood and met the first female pastor I'd ever known, I realized I could finally be what I'd always known God was calling me to be!"

Even decades after the first women were ordained in 1970, many women continue to face resistance from both their biological family and their church families when they begin conversations about discerning a call to ministry. One woman summed up what many experienced: "I was very anxious about 'coming out' about my sense of call to the ministry." Another woman says that when she told her family she was going to seminary, her mother did not talk to her for days. "My parents were not risk-takers. She saw this as a risk. I was throwing away a good job and any chance for a marriage and children." Several women similarly said that their families' immediate response was disappointment that their daughter would, they presumed, never marry. And two of the women I interviewed shared having a grandparent offer to pay for an older brother to go to seminary (and in both cases he did *not* go) and then not offering to help when they went. Whereas for many families having a son go into the ministry is a source of pride, having a daughter in ministry can be disorienting or even shameful. Perhaps this is why some women shared stories of families who seemed to willfully misunderstand what they meant when they first talked to them about seminary. One woman, for example, said that when she told her family she was going to be ordained, her grandmother's first—and most persistent question—was "So, you're interested in Christian education?" Her grandmother, she said, "always assumed that was the goal; she simply could not (or would not) entertain the possibility that a woman would serve in any other capacity within the church."

Pastors and congregations are not always any more supportive than parents and families. One woman who had been a very active lay leader in her congregation said that when she announced to the congregation (many of whom were struggling with the reality that the congregation had recently called its first female pastor) that she was going to seminary, the announcement was "met with absolute silence." And another woman, who was working in youth and family ministry (as a lay leader), was hesitant to talk with the senior pastor of the congregation about her desire to go to seminary. "When I finally did tell him—because I had told the women's circle (all of whom said essentially, "Well, it's about time!")—he was not supportive. He didn't really say he didn't think I should do it, he just didn't offer any encouragement. Though he says he supports women in ministry, I don't think he really does." This quiet lack of support from pastors seems to be more common than outright discouragement (nearly half of the women interviewed shared such nonresponses), but a number of interviewed pastors did report also having been told early on by their pastors that being a female pastor would be challenging. One woman says, that when she spoke with her home pastor, he told her: "Lots of congregations in this part of the country [the South] will accept a female pastor only if they have a *real* pastor too." He then told her, "You may go through all of this [candidacy and seminary] and end up in a dying congregation in South Dakota." The women who were told things like this all acknowledged an assumption that the pastor was trying to be helpful by offering what he saw as a realistic perspective. But surprisingly few expressed having experienced strong support from their own pastors.

Despite the lack of encouragement, despite puzzlement, despite family tension, and occasional blatant misogyny, the women repeatedly shared stories of God's grace and of a call that is too persistent, too big, and too right to ignore. One woman said that her own experience of hearing and receiving God's grace, of having been forgiven, was so powerful that she "wanted to share it with others. I knew I was called to ministry. And I knew that meant ordained ministry. Regardless of obstacles." Another woman said that in the midst of a period of time in her life when she was trying to hear God's voice, she went on a mission trip. During an evening worship she was asked to assist with communion. "I got to say 'The blood of Christ shed for you,' and I realized I could do *this* forever." She knew then that she was called to do precisely that.

A few of the women whose fathers were pastors who had supported their sense of call into the ministry describe their call process as one which strengthened their families. One in particular said that her father was a voting member of the Lutheran Church in America (LCA) Assembly in 1970 when the assembly approved women's ordination. Shortly afterwards she began her journey to seminary, and he "later preached for my ordination. It was an incredible gift to both of us." Unfortunately stories were rare of calls and ordinations of daughters and granddaughters bringing families together. But for the women who had such stories, the power of receiving a blessing on their calling from their pastor-fathers was clearly very meaningful.

## Ecclesial Voices

For the vast majority of the pastors interviewed, candidacy was an overwhelmingly positive experience of discernment and an affirmation of gifts. However a few notable—but instructive—exceptions were mentioned. A number of people said they experienced some pushback because they were single. One felt resistance because she was lesbian. Another faced scrutiny because "candidacy was fixated on my sexual orientation." Even though this pastor is straight and single, because she had written in her candidacy paperwork that she was "hoping for a partner to share my life with," her candidacy committee was "concerned that I was gay." She said the more candidacy pushed her to elaborate on this, the more it felt inappropriate, so the stronger she resisted.

Another pastor described a candidacy process that did not follow the "normal" order and time frame. She said her candidacy committee was very difficult to work with, and that she almost left the process as a result. The "problems" were that she had gone to seminary before entering the candidacy process—and thus without candidacy approval—and that she had already been working as a hospital chaplain. She expressed frustration, not so much with the "hoops" of candidacy, but with what she experienced as a double standard. "I have a female colleague who, like me, had to fight with the candidacy committee because we didn't follow their prescribed formula. But I have a male colleague with a very similar story who was praised, *by a member of the bishop's staff* for being entrepreneurial." Several women expressed frustration that when women do not neatly fit the candidacy mold, they are seen as problems to be solved. However, when men do not fit the mold, they are seen as taking initiative.

Despite these inappropriately difficult candidacy experiences, most of the pastors remember their candidacy process as a very positive one. Most of the pastors likewise report very positive experiences with faculty in seminary—but not necessarily with their student colleagues. A significant number of women recalled experiences of harassment and misogyny from peers. "We had male colleagues routinely saying that women should not be pastors. One said things like 'women who want to be pastors all have daddy issues.'" Another woman who had her first child during internship related that a male student had said that women shouldn't be pastors "because they were 'clinically insane' after giving birth." When I asked if these conversations were taking place inside or outside classrooms, I was told:

> These men would try to trick faculty into saying that women should not be ordained. One faculty member, in response, said that only the church fathers really spoke

against women's ordination, suggesting that was less a theological or interpretative question but rather one of culture and chronology. Not ten minutes later, talking about something completely different, he stressed how important the church fathers were for the church today. I don't think he had any sense of what he had just done.

Another woman shared about having gone to a faculty member to ask for assistance in navigating this territory. The faculty member was very supportive and "tried to be helpful. But the faculty could not change this attitude." Several of the pastors shared being made very uncomfortable, resentful, and even anxious, by the reality that they now served in communities with male colleagues who had made their disapproval of women in ministry so obvious when they had been in seminary together. "It is especially difficult to watch them 'ladder climb' and 'steeple chase' in the synod so successfully."

For many female candidates, first call is a completely different—and more challenging—experience than candidacy and seminary.[3] And this difference is one that judicatory officials are acutely

3. The first call process in the ELCA is slightly different from any subsequent calls. During a candidate's final year of candidacy—which is typically also the candidate's final year of seminary—they are assigned to one of the nine ELCA regions. The regions are made up of multiple synods and grouped geographically. This study, for example, was focused on most of Region 9 (the Southeast) and part of Region 4 (the central and south-central part of the US). Then the candidate is assigned to a particular synod within that Region.

The call process varies slightly from synod to synod, but generally speaking, the bishop's office will send a candidate's name and paperwork to congregations in the call process that are deemed appropriate places for a first-call (new) pastor to serve. Unlike bishops the United Methodist Church, ELCA bishops do not simply assign a pastor to a congregation. The bishop (or bishop's designee working with call process) tries to match the gifts of individual pastors with the needs of particular congregations. The bishop's office typically sends a set number—often three or four—names of pastors to each congregation in the call process. The congregation's call committee is then responsible for the interview process. A candidate typically has one or two interviews with a call committee, and if the call committee and the candidate both feel that this may, in fact, be a call from God, the candidate's name is given to the congregational council. At this point the council may choose to meet with the candidate. If this meeting confirms the call committee's sense that this candidate is the right

aware of. More than a dozen of the pastors I interviewed recalled having been told by the bishop in the synod they were originally assigned to that getting a call was much more challenging for women than for men.[4] And many of these women remembered their dismay at the matter-of-factness of their bishop's statement. "It was as if," one woman told me, "he was detached from the process and could not do anything about it. But I didn't buy it then and I certainly don't buy it now." One judicatory official told me that in their synod it takes on average three months longer for women to receive a first call than it does men, and the starting pay package is considerably less than what is offered to their male counterparts—anecdotally as much as ten thousand dollars per year less.[5]

Several of the bishops I interviewed said they make sure that all congregations receive a slate of potential candidates that includes both men and women. "The challenge is," one bishop told me, "will they get a second interview? Sometimes they get a perfunctory Skype interview to satisfy our requirement, and then the call committee just moves on." Another bishop said that roughly one-quarter of the active pastors in the synod are female, so the synod strives to make sure that every slate is one quarter female. "Twenty-five percent feels

---

pastor for the congregation, the council will often set a time for the candidate to meet the congregation. Shortly after this meeting, the congregation will vote on the candidate in a called congregational meeting.

If the vote is favorable, the congregational council will extend a call to the candidate. And if the candidate accepts the call, an ordination date will be set. Candidates in the ELCA cannot be ordained until receiving a call to serve a congregation.

4. This was said to women assigned to synods across the United States, not just in the South.

5. Though an exact answer to how long the first call process takes on average is hard to determine, I asked the assistants to the bishops in the synods where I interviewed to give me an estimate. Their estimates varied from five to seven months on average. And they also each said that it was not uncommon for women and minorities to take considerably longer. It is even more difficult to discern (but equally interesting) how much longer women spend, on average, than men in the call process in subsequent calls. And if the answer is that it is sometimes nearly impossible for a female pastor to receive a subsequent call, as I suspect it is, this would result in female pastors being disproportionately "stuck" in unhealthy calls where they are underpaid.

low to me, but I know this is actually up from just a few years ago. We've been very intentional. But it can be hard because we simply don't have enough female candidates." But the reality is that women make up roughly half of all seminarians. And this has been true for the past two decades. So, if there are not enough women in the synods, it is at least in part because they have been unable to get a first call and thus have not been ordained.

And when the bishops and bishops' staffs in charge of the call process required that every slate a congregation receives has a mix of men and women on the slate, they often got pushback from the call committee or congregational council. One bishop said some congregations routinely complain—if he sends them a slate of four candidates with two men and two women (or, heaven forbid, one man and three women)—that there are too many women on the slate. The bishop's response: "Would we be having this conversation if the genders were reversed? And if not, then why are we having it now?!" The bishops who are most insistent that congregations will receive women candidates also often have to insist that *all* of the candidates be interviewed before a congregation can reject a slate. Several bishops and assistants to bishops shared stories of call committees and ultimately congregations that changed their stance on female pastors after call committees were told that they had to meet with a female candidate.

However, not all bishops insist on a female candidate on every slate. Several bishops report not being willing to "fight" with a congregation on this issue in part because they imagine it will do more harm than good to the women in the process. One bishop with this approach shared a story of a surprising reversal. He had sent an all-male slate of candidates to a congregation that had plainly stated that they would refuse to even interview a female pastor. After several interviews the church council chair asked the bishop why the congregation had not been sent any female names. The bishop told the (male) council chair, "I'm not willing to subject anyone to what would be inevitable failure." Well, the bishop was told, it had been only the call committee chair who had been opposed to a female candidate. In the end the bishop did send a female candidate—the person he had thought was the best fit for the congregation from the beginning—and the congregation called her. And, the bishop reports, it has been a great call for both. Several judicatory officials likewise suggested that all too often (perhaps the majority of the time), the refusal to interview a female pastoral candidate stems from only one or two people—almost always straight, white, and male (but sometimes older and female with significant social clout)—who assume a certain level of power, privilege, and authority, and who are willing to dominate and bully the rest of the committee and maybe even the entire congregation.

Quite a few of the female pastors told stories of terribly stressful first call experiences. One tells of having interviewed in a congregation she was already serving as an interim. Because she had already graduated from seminary, and because the congregation was geographically remote and finding supply pastors was challenging, the bishop had given her a dispensation to preside over communion.[6] She felt like the interview process, though much longer and more deliberate than anticipated, had been going well. And then she was told, "We're just not sure we're ready for a female pastor." The bishop thanked her for her service to the congregation and told her that because of the congregation's great experience with her, even though they had not called her, she would have laid the foundation for them to eventually consider calling a woman. "But," she said, "you get damn tired of being the example."

Another pastor shared a similar experience of a first-call interview process: it seemed to be going well, but the call committee also seemed to be dragging its feet. The pastor said she was pretty sure the hesitation was because she was a woman. She said she really wanted to ask the call committee chair this question directly but the assistant to the bishop in charge of call process asked her

6. Only ordained pastors preside over communion in the ELCA. However, bishops can make exceptions to this, allowing someone who is not (yet) ordained to preside over communion in extenuating circumstances such as when a congregation—especially a small rural congregation—would otherwise go for an extended period of time without communion. This most often happens in situations similar to this one where an intern or interim who is not yet ordained is serving in lieu of an ordained pastor.

not to, told her to wait, to make them actually say it. "Finally they did. We were at lunch during our fifth (!!) and, it turned out, final interview when a member of the committee said to me: 'You are perfect for us. The only problem is that you are a woman.'"

Quite a few women reported taking over a year to receive a first call. Many of them were openly told it was because they were women. Some congregations couched their rejections in terms of their concerns about the candidate fitting in: concerns ran the gamut—from the candidate's lack of family in the area to a lack of childcare resources in the community to the possibility that the candidate might become pregnant and leave the congregation without a pastor to the eventuality that a married candidate's husband either might be unable to find a job in the area or might be unwilling to move for his wife's vocation to the prospect that an unmarried candidate might become too lonely to remain long in whatever community the church was in. These experiences are "normal" in that they are quite common; they are not aberrations. One of the bishops told me that a queer female pastor told him she experienced considerably more discrimination based on her gender than her sexual orientation. He said this initially surprised him, but in time he has come to see that in the church it can be "much harder to be female than to be queer."

All the women I interviewed did, in fact, receive a first call. But even those that were received were often quite bumpy. A number of women recounted that they accepted their first calls in order to be ordained, even after the margins of congregational votes in their favor were considerably narrower than they imagined their male colleagues would have been willing to accept. They hoped they would be able to change the hearts and minds of the people once they were in office, and that a second call, were they to need to leave, would be less challenging. But many of these contested first calls resulted in a drastic reduction of church membership. One pastor I interviewed said that a member of the call committee told the rest of the committee, "I believe she is called to be the pastor here. And when she is called, we will be leaving because we don't believe women should be pastors." This committee member seemed to have no recognition of the disconnect within his statement, and the entire family did indeed leave before the new pastor's first Sunday.

Another pastor said that a man who had made it clear that he had not voted for her looked sick during worship one Sunday, and left the sanctuary looking pained during the sermon. After the service she went to check on the man, thinking she may need to call for help and he told her that hearing a woman preach had made him physically sick. He and his family left the congregation after that. "Knowing people have left because I was called—that I have caused pain—is my greatest challenge and my deepest sorrow." Nearly every single pastor I interviewed mentioned knowing that some have left every church they have served, often without meeting her, simply because she is female. And nearly every single pastor I interviewed expressed a sense of sorrow, but also shame, because of this.

One pastor recollected that right as worship was about to begin and she was in the narthex with the choir and the acolytes, ready to process, a middle-aged male visitor came in. He looked around, realized that the woman he was looking at was the pastor, said loudly, "Nope, not for me!" and walked out. As bad as this was, what was worse was that she then heard an usher "whisper" to another member, "Well, I guess that's what we get for hiring a woman."

And such responses are not restricted to men. Several pastors report that their most challenging critics are middle-aged and older women. I asked a few of the pastors why they thought this was. "I think some are jealous. They see me doing something they couldn't do. Maybe they can't say that outright. But it shapes our interactions." Another pastor said she knows that she is perceived as "intimidating" by some, perhaps especially by older female parishioners "who have been socialized to be more demure" than she is. But, the same pastor said that younger parishioners—whether male or female—don't seem to share this struggle, making her wonder if it is more generational than anything.

Several judicatory officials, much like the bishop I mentioned above, commented on the need for the "first" woman to serve a church so that a congregation can have a positive experience of female pastoral leadership. The overwhelming majority of the women in this study were in at least one call that first woman. And quite a few of the pastors have been that first woman in each call they have accepted. Many of them, like the pastor above, express a level of fatigue with always being the first. One woman expressed feeling like something of a zoo exhibit. And yet most of the women who have served as the first female pastor know they have changed—hopefully forever—the minds and hearts of the members of the congregations they have served. I heard dozens of versions of an older member—usually, but not always, male—telling the female pastor after some time, "I was opposed to calling you as our pastor because you're a woman, but I am so glad we got you."

## "Lower Your Voice, Please . . ."

The challenges of women in the parish do not end once they are called. One bishop remarked, "I see female clergy doing a fantastic job even though the odds are stacked against them. Even though it is less a 'man's world' than it used to be, their voices still tend to be drowned out." Another bishop echoed this sense: "I struggle with this as bishop. I try to address it. I know there are significantly less women in ministry, but even so, their voices are often simply not attended to." Female pastors, likewise, often feel unheard both in their congregations and in the synod.

Another judicatory official, in speaking of the conference dean meetings said that in his synod conferences elect their own deans (they are not appointed by the bishop), and that the male conference deans outnumber the female deans by five to one. The bishop notes that he observes the men routinely talking "over" the women and, he says, they use not only their voices but their bodies to do so. "I want to ask them to learn how to modulate their voices and bearing so that their sisters can be heard."

This bishop recalled that he got the idea of asking his male colleagues to modulate their voices from an experience at a Conference of Bishops gathering. At the time of this particular gathering there were eleven female and fifty-five male bishops. So, the men in worship outnumbered the women five to one. (This is an exaggerated reversal of what most congregations experience on a given Sunday morning, when women significantly outnumber men.) While the group was singing during worship, one of the male bishops noticed that the men's voices were completely drowning out the women's voices. He called this to the attention of the whole assembly and asked that the men pay more attention and modulate their singing so that the women's voices could be heard. The bishop who shared this story with me said he found such noticing to be such a helpful and informative exercise. "What a great exercise in awareness! It made me wonder how often we [the church] fail to attend to women's voices."[7]

One judicatory official noted that women's responses to their relative lack of voice and influence

> seems to be experienced differently by the older generation of female pastors and younger. Because the older generation never expected equality, they are just grateful for a seat at the table. But younger women know they could be doctors, lawyers, etc. They—rightly—expect to be treated equally and are not. They get mad about it.

One of the younger pastors I spoke with said that she finds herself so tired of being talked over by male colleagues, especially when she is the only woman in a clergy gathering, that she has learned to say, "Please do not interrupt me." Most of her colleagues, she says, apologize and seem to make an effort to be more attentive to her voice after such a conversation. But, she said, she has "one colleague in particular who appears to be offended by my offense." She, like many of her colleagues, expressed how exhausting it is to feel like you are always either having to teach others how to treat you or having to accept mistreatment.

Many of the women, regardless of age, expressed the sense that it is our cultural presumptions about leadership that create the conflict for women. As one woman said, "I don't want to be

---

7. This story is shared with the permission of both the bishop who first shared it with me and the bishop who suggested the exercise.

perpetuating stereotypes, but Western civilization has trained us to listen to louder, bigger, more boisterous voices. We have to learn how to listen to quieter leadership, leadership which may actually be even stronger." Women's voices, in other words, are often drowned out because they are softer but also because we have been trained to attend to male voices over female voices. One pastor shared having been asked to lead a particular event in her conference. One of her male colleagues arrived late but walked in and immediately took over the conversation. He simply talked over her. She shared that in the moment she knew she "should call him on it. But I couldn't. Because I know—we all know—that to make a man like that angry, to embarrass him in front of people, would only make things bad for me in the long run." And, as she said, everyone in the room would listen to him because "he could and would be louder."

Though women do typically have higher-pitched voices than men do, volume is not an inherently physical, gendered characteristic. Many, if not most, women were taught to be quieter. "Good girls are quiet and calm, and always put others' needs and concerns first" is the lesson several pastors shared having internalized growing up. "I was taught to be quiet. To be good. To be nice. To be submissive. Learning to speak out has been—and will no doubt continue to be—a lifelong journey for me." And another woman said, "It took me decades to learn that I had my own voice. But it is still very difficult to use it. I guess I'm still afraid to." And quiet voices are often equated to a level of sweetness that is not asked of male pastors (or of men in general). As one pastor said, "People want me to be a professional nice person. But I'm not always nice. And people expect me to be sweeter than they would if I were male. This expectation does *not* engender sweetness or niceness in me."

The images of traditional gender roles in which women are quiet and sweet also keep women at home in the collective imagination. "There are tapes in my head from my mother's generation. They are not telling me *not* to be a pastor. But they are telling me that I should be taking care of my house, my husband, and my kids." It is the implicit messages of what it means to be a "good" wife and mother, and the collective assumption that this is what women are called to, that often shapes the response to women in ministry. A clinging to what is perceived as traditional and stable— a nostalgic desire for what "used to be"—can actively silence any voices that are perceived as a threat. As one judicatory official said, "I would have expected resistance to women in ministry to have decreased by now, but it hasn't. In fact, I think it has increased in times of high anxiety . . . After 2009 and with economic stresses . . . Congregations that are anxious about survival don't want to take a risk." And female pastors are at least perceived as being politically and socially risky for many congregations.

Quite a few of the pastors I interviewed talked about ways they had used traditional notions of femininity to flip the script on/for members of the congregation who remained obviously opposed to their role in the church. One pastor said that there had been an older man in the congregation she currently serves who for months would not take communion if she was presiding. He would only commune when the male senior pastor presided. And he had made it clear that it was because he could not—in his words—take communion from a woman. The church was in the meantime struggling with a groundhog on the property. The older man stopped by the church in the midst of this, and on a day when the male senior pastor was not there. The female pastor asked him to kill the groundhog for her. "Since then he seems to accept me as his pastor, and now he takes communion from me." She said she thinks her request righted whatever he had felt was wrong in their relationship and that by inviting him into a role that aligned with his own sense of masculinity, she had affirmed him. Now their relationship is, she says, much better, and he seems to respect her authority as pastor.

Several pastors who started ministry outside the South and moved into the area have expressed exacerbation at all the gendered problems once they moved south. "Coming to the South was terrible," one woman said. "It was like going back in time twenty years." And a number of the pastors from other areas express feeling as if their lack of Southernness both hurts and helps them in ministry. Some said they know they do not fit in, they do not in-tuitively behave like they are expected to behave as women, and they realize this has alienated them from many members of their congregations and of their communities.

But others have found ways to use their nonnative voices cre-atively when challenged. One pastor tells of having been stopped as she was getting on a hospital elevator wearing a clerical collar. A man asked her if she was a "lady pastor." She responded, "Yes, I am a pastor." He then asked her what she did with Saint Paul. She asked what he did with Dorcas and Phoebe. "They weren't ordained," he answered. "And neither was Paul." She said as she stepped off of the elevator. As she related this story she mused, this would not have happened to her husband—also a pastor—and, she said, "Things like this only happened once we moved to the South. I feel like we've move back in time thirty years. And it does not serve me well." As we talked about this story, she reflected that she did not feel that she often responded very gracefully to such attacks on her call, and she lamented the failure to engage in what might more likely be a transformative conversation. And yet, who knows what this man heard or took away from this conversation. I like to imagine that he remained on the elevator, contemplating what she had said. Perhaps he heard her voice precisely because the encounter was brief and nonpersonal, and therefore nonthreatening.

Cultural expectations for women do not remain in the church and community but extend to the home as well. Numerous stud-ies suggest that within professional heterosexual couples, working women carry a considerably larger percentage of the housework and childcare load than men. Quite a few of the female pastors expressed frustration at very unbalanced expectations. Perhaps because women who were part of a clergy couple have greater per-sonal expectations for a degree of equity regarding work/life bal-ance, and perhaps because they have a much greater understanding of exactly what it is their husbands are doing at work, female pastors married to male pastors expressed greater frustration with imbal-ance at home when it exists than did the female pastors married to professionals in other fields. As one female pastor who is part of a clergy couple said, "There are always unspoken expectations, both at church and at home. The partner balance has always been a tremendous stress. I've disappointed a lot of people in any given day. Sometimes my family because of the stuff I do for the church. And sometimes the church because of the stuff I do for my family." Concrete examples of expectations on female pastors, which several women offered, were that the female pastors (not the male pastors) would contribute to potlucks, would help clean the church, and would assist in childcare during church events. Their husbands, also pastors, they overwhelmingly agreed, simply do not have to meet these same expectations. So, since the expectations are so lopsided, "I'm set up to fail and he is set up to succeed." Or, she is set up to remain exhausted while he is encouraged to "take your day off, Pastor," because he is perceived as always going above and beyond while she is perceived as never doing enough, despite clear evidence that she carries the greater workload.

Out of eighty-five women interviewed, only a very, very few (and notably they were each in clergy couples) put forth a counternarrative. One woman, for example, who has always served with her spouse in ministry says, "We have always split everything equally—parenting, pastoring, chores. It has been great for us. And hopefully a good model for others." But she is acutely aware that this is not the norm. For the women who are part of a clergy couple in which the work is shouldered more or less evenly, the benefits are great. These women report enjoying both their ministry and their home life and feeling supported in both.

Many women serve on a male/female ministry team with male colleagues. Most often this means that the female pastor is serving as an associate pastor with a male senior pastor. Male and female ministry colleagues who are not married to each other have a completely different dynamic from clergy couples serving together, but the division of labor still often falls along traditionally conceived gender lines: the male pastor has more public roles of preaching (especially at high-attendance events such as Christmas Eve or Easter Sunday worship services) and community events, and the female pastor often takes responsibility for education, children's ministry, and pastoral care. One female associate pastor who works with a younger male senior pastor said that the senior pastor openly and often tells members of the congregation, "I don't do pastoral care; that's her job." I have not been able to find studies on the "emotional labor" of ministry and what role gender plays; however, a number of studies have been done in academia that suggest that female faculty members in colleges and universities do a disproportionate amount of the emotional labor (counseling and student advising as well as caregiving for colleagues) such that it is detrimental to both their professional lives (time spent caregiving is time not spent researching and writing) and to their own mental and emotional well-being (it is exhausting).[8] Based on my interviews with female associate pastors working with male senior pastors, I think the same thing is happening in congregations. This, it seems, is an important thing for bishops and bishops' staffs to know as they work (and I know in many congregations this is an ongoing focus) to prepare more women for leadership positions in larger congregations, in synodical leadership, or both.

## Lonely in the Wilderness

One of the most common emotions shared by women in ministry is loneliness. Many of our female pastors are the only women in ministry in their community. Many are the first woman in the context of their current call. Many have literally given all they have—sometimes losing the support of family along the way, precisely because of their dedication to following Christ's call into the ministry—to be where they are. They are intensely lonely. "I've had to work really, really hard not to be lonely. I can't be friends with members of the congregation. And unlike my male counterparts, I don't fit anywhere in the local clergy groups as I've almost always been the only female clergy in town." Though many women do report strong relationships with local male colleagues, they experience ministry as still largely a "good ol' boy" system in frequent

8. Guarino and Bordon, "Faculty Service Loads," 672–94.

and profound ways. For example, several women shared being intentionally excluded from clergy groups that work together for confirmation because they are women.

Because of their loneliness, some of the pastors shared that it is really hard to maintain appropriate boundaries with their parishioners. Holiday meals, birthday celebrations, invitations to dinner and social events become blurry. "Because I am single and no longer have children at home, I work all the time. I'm lonely. Work gives me something to do. But I know I need to set better boundaries." These blurred boundaries may not lead to boundary violations—in fact, I suspect they seldom if ever do—but they may make effective ministry more challenging, further isolating these pastors. This problem is much deeper and more prevalent than I suspect most male colleagues (pastors or bishops) realize.

One male judicatory official shared with me the first time he realized just how differently he experienced the lived reality of ministry than did his female colleagues. His first call was as an associate pastor working with a female senior pastor. He was told by a number of his male clergy colleagues and friends that he was crazy for being willing to work with—and under—"that woman." He described her as "very bright and very driven"—traits, he pointed out, the same colleagues would have praised in a male colleague. In fact, such traits would have made a male colleague "a good bishop." These men did not know what to do with a woman they perceived as uncharacteristically aggressive. Still, the current bishop enjoyed working with her in his first call: he found her energizing and empowering. So one day he asked her, "What has your experience in ministry been like?" And she started to cry. "I've been doing this for more than twenty years. And I'm good at it. And yet I am still only barely tolerated. I am unbearably lonely." He says this interaction and the deepening relationship between the two of them continues to shape him profoundly. "I realize I simply cannot imagine some of the experiences my female colleagues have had and continue to have."

And it is true that male colleagues and bishops cannot imagine the experiences of their female colleagues. But they can learn to hear their stories, believe them, and respond appropriately. One female pastor told me this: "I'm so lonely sometimes that I'm terribly depressed. I've reached out to the bishop's staff several times, even asking for help in my confidential report to the bishop. But I've received no pastoral help, no check in. No response. I feel brushed off and unimportant." Many of the church's female pastors, like this woman, are crying out, and yet they remain largely unheard.

## Suggested Resources

Leach, Tara Beth. *Emboldened: A Vision for Empowering Women in Ministry.* Downers Grove, IL: InterVarsity, 2017.
Lewis, Karoline M. *She: Five Keys to Unlock the Power of Women in Ministry.* Nashville: Abingdon, 2016.

## Discussion Questions

1. What voices are not being heard in your church or community? How might your community be missing the voice of the Spirit?

2. How can you support the hearing of women's voices in your church, workplace, school, and community?

3. Do you think congregations should be allowed to decide whether or not to interview pastors based on gender? (Or, for that matter, race or sexual orientation?) Why or why not?

4. Have you been in situations where you had no voice? What is that like?

5. How equally is emotional labor shared in your home or workplace?

# 3

# Embodying Ministry

In 2014, Tina Fey's *Bossypants* struck a chord with many; in part because Fey is hilarious, but also because every professional woman—perhaps every woman!—can relate to Fey's account of being a woman in a position of leadership and being asked, consistently and with some degree of disbelief, what it's like to be in a position of authority. "Is it uncomfortable for you to be the person in charge?" "You know, in the same way they say, 'Gosh, Mr. Trump, is it awkward for you to be the boss of all these people?'"[1] The suggestion that women do—and should—struggle with images of themselves as "in charge" and that men do not—and should not—is merely the beginning of the cultural gender norms Fey takes aim at. Fey also offers advice to "bossypants" women: outwork and outpace those who don't like you being in charge. "Then, when you're in charge, don't hire the people who were jerky to you."[2] Being a pastor isn't exactly the same as being an executive producer. And female pastors have to continue to work with—and share God's love with—those members of the congregations they serve whether they were jerky to them or not. Fey promises that "opinions will change organically when you're the boss. Or they won't. Who cares?"[3] But we—people, women, even Tina Fey—do care.

Fey's book is funny because it reflects the gendered cultural reality we live in, a reality in which any woman who asserts herself

1. Fey, *Bossypants*, 5.
2. Fey, *Bossypants*, 130.
3. Fey, *Bossypants*, 131.

is called bossy or worse. This gendered cultural reality is in the church as much as it is in the media. Women continue to be called names for standing up for themselves, for advocating for causes they feel strongly about, and for having personal ambitions. Women, in other words, are called names for behavior that is not only praised in but expected of men. This experience of name-calling does not merely reflect the culture, however, it reinforces and creates the reality in which we live.

## Feminine Stereotypes and Archetypes

The popular children's toys GI Joe and Barbie offer a glimpse into the cultural gendered norms that shape (and/or reflect) our collective expectations of men and women. GI Joe, first of all, is not marketed as a doll. He is an action figure. In other words GI Joe (and thus the little boy who plays with him) is created to *do* things. And he has a body that suggests that the things he does are big, powerful, important things. Barbie, on the other hand, is indeed a doll. She is *not* an action figure. In fact, her figure itself suggests that action is minimal; even walking appears to be a challenge for Barbie. Studies have shown that Barbie warps girls' body image.[4] She creates unreasonable (and impractical) beauty standards all while teaching little girls that looking beautiful and shopping a lot is what women do. The subtlety of this education of gender norms makes it all the more insidious. Precisely because they are largely unspoken, they are absorbed by children much like language is.

These cultural expectations do not remain on the elementary school playground. Women have been taught—both explicitly and implicitly—to be sweet and quiet. To be nurturing and maternal. To be gentle and calm. To be attractive and fashionable. To be lady-like. And when women behave in ways that challenge these cultural expectations, they are called bossy, feisty, abrasive, frumpy, bitchy, and worse. Often these expectations and norms are turned into humor. For example, Dave Ramsey, a Christian financial advisor with

4. See, for example, Wolf, *Beauty Myth.*

a popular radio show and other platforms, says that couples need to work together to make financial decisions. In one rant captured on YouTube, Ramsey says that the last thing a husband needs during financial stress "is a barking Chihuahua around his ankles."[5] Though Ramsey uses humor rather than crude language, he essentially says that when women are assertive they are bitches. But we are also taught that when men are assertive they are good leaders.

This is precisely the message female pastors receive while at the very same time being held accountable for leading a congregation. Many pastors feel this a something of a catch-22. "If I don't 'lead like a man,' I'm weak and a failure. And if I do, I'm a bitch." Or, "I'm told I need to have more of a backbone. Not to let the bullies on council run over me. But I'm also told I need to smile more." Quite a few pastors I interviewed said they've been told to smile more. "You're too pretty not to smile." "You'd be less intimidating if you'd smile more." Whether intentional or not, for many women the perception of their leadership ability is directly connected to their appearance and demeanor, where traditional (read, nonthreatening) understandings of femininity are good and anything else is unacceptable.

When bodied language is used to describe personality traits the language almost always denigrates the female body while holding up the male body, even if crudely, as the standard for leadership. This standard is next to impossible for a woman to meet and is one for which she is judged as somehow or other failing to be a "good" woman if she does.

We do inhabit the world in particular bodies, bodies that are male or female.[6] And the particularity of our bodies matters. When women fail (or refuse) to accommodate their behavior and demeanor to the cultural expectations associated with the female

5. Ramsey, "Marriage and Money."

6. This is, of course, not an objectively true claim. There are intersex people who are born with characteristics that are both male and female. And the LGBTQIA+ community continues to raise our collective awareness of the problems with understanding sexuality in such a strict binary. On the whole, however, we respond to, and are responded to by, others based in large part on our perceived gender—male or female.

body, they often become the objects of bodied criticisms. Several women shared having stood up to someone within the congregation or on the council and being told by others that they were "ballsy." These comments came from men in a tone of respect and admiration mixed with a bit of disbelief. And several women, after having gone toe-to-toe with powerful (usually male) members of their congregations or communities have heard of the "pissing contests" in which they engaged. One woman shared having received a water gun in the shape of a penis as a gift from female colleagues so she would be better equipped for such contests in the future.

Every woman I interviewed recognized the delicacy of this balance, not only for themselves, but for the sake of every other female pastor. The overwhelming majority of women interviewed expressed recognition that in many interactions with others they are—surprisingly often—the first and perhaps only female pastor or religious leader someone has ever met. These folks often doubt they have understood correctly:

"So, you're like a girl priest."

"Well, sort of. I'm an ELCA pastor and I happen to be a woman."

Or, "Oh wow! I've heard of women pastors before, but I've never actually *seen* one." Women have been ordained in the ELCA for almost fifty years, and yet female pastors are often still treated as novelties, even in ELCA settings. Given the relative novelty of female pastors, those around them are far more likely to generalize about their experiences of women (or of African Americans, Latin@s, or members of the LGBTQ community) than they might about their experiences of white men. "This puts lots of pressure on minorities—it has exhausted many of the female pastors I know. They have stories of deep pain—real wounds—from this experience."

Knowing that one is always acting as a representative for all women everywhere can be both exhausting and demoralizing. This is even more true for women of color and for those who do not identify as straight and cisgendered. This truth is felt more strongly when someone has had a previous negative (or even neutral) experience with a woman in a position of power. A number of congregations will say, "We had a woman before and we had a problem . . . So we don't want another woman." Whatever they have experienced with one female pastor they assume of all. This does not happen with male pastors. Congregations realize that all male pastors are individuals with unique gifts and strengths and quirks and foibles. And yet they persist in assuming that any given woman is a representative for the whole. One of the male bishops told me that he regularly calls congregations on this when they tell him they don't want a female pastor because of a negative previous experience.

"You've had both good and bad male pastors, right? And yet you've never told me you didn't want a male pastor because of a bad previous experience."

He says they often respond with nods of affirmation and continue to insist that the congregation "needs" a male pastor to counteract the previous negative experience with a female pastor.

Because they recognize the importance of experience with a "good" female pastor, several judicatory officials reported intentionally sending women whom they viewed as particularly strong pastors to supply preach or to serve as interims in congregations resistant to female clergy. Said one, "Exposure and positive experience of healthy leadership from a strong female pastor often builds the bridges folks need." In a sense, this strategy uses the tendency to generalize in the favor of female pastors. A judicatory official went on to say that after a positive interim experience with a female pastor in a congregation, members of a call committee were more easily convinced to at least interview a female candidate.[7] "We've actually never had a congregation refuse a female interim, even congregations that would never call a female pastor." Because the congregations do not say no to a female interim, having a positive experience with an interim female pastor helps congregations to develop an image of pastor that is not exclusively white and male. It sometimes opens them—theoretically, at least—to the possibility of having a

7. As I am writing this, some of the synods are shifting their practices. One of the synods in the purview of this study is now committed to using all female clergy for the call committee mock interviews so that the call committee members have experiences with female pastors whether they choose to interview one or not.

full-called female pastor down the road. Knowing that this is what is happening adds yet another layer of responsibility to the already stress-filled position of the women serving in this capacity.

A few of the male bishops acknowledged realizing that they, too, have sometimes been guilty of generalizing about female pastors in ways that they simply would not about male pastors. One bishop recalled that when he was a parish pastor, a female seminary intern had called him on his assumptions. He had had a negative experience with a female intern previously. In his words the first intern was "not a disaster, but she lacked interpersonal skills and didn't connect with the folks in the congregation." During the seminary supervising pastor/intern interviews, he told a prospective female intern that the congregation "needed" a male intern to "get over" the negative experience. The interviewing seminarian made it clear that he should not lump all women into one model. She asked him, "What makes you think women pastors are all the same? Did it ever dawn on you that two women pastors may be completely different !?" He went on to reflect, "She really challenged me. You have an assumption that one bad experience with a female pastor means you don't like female pastors—but you've had negative experiences with a male pastor and not dismissed male pastors." This pastor/bishop says he shares this story with others, including call committees, in the hopes that he can help others rethink their practice without shaming them.

That both individuals and congregations generalize their experiences with female pastors in a way that they do not with male pastors adds to the reality that women cannot get away with being good. They have to be *better*. Male pastors (especially white, straight, married male pastors with two or three children) are almost always given the benefit of the doubt. As long as they are not a disaster (in other words, as long as they avoid sexual misconduct and financial malfeasance), they are perceived as being "good enough." But for a woman to be "good enough" requires that she stand in the place of all women to win over those who enter into an interaction predisposed to find fault with a female pastor in principle.

## Women as Unclean

Lev 15:19–31 is at least in some part responsible for the institutional resistance to women in ministry. This is true even though few would be able or willing to give voice to it. This passage in Leviticus declares that women are ritually unclean during their menstrual cycles. This uncleanness means that everything they touch is likewise rendered unclean. Thus, because they have had, are having, or will have a menstrual cycle, girls and women are deemed unclean and thus unfit for the holy work of the priesthood. Given the givenness (thank you, God) of menstrual cycles and assumptions about the scriptural author, the logical conclusion is that it is *God* who deems women unclean.[8] And, given the givenness of menstrual cycles, there is nothing a woman can do to make herself clean/worthy of approaching the altar of God.

During the time I was doing research for this book, I heard from a young woman about an older, white male biology professor who told his students that precisely because women have menstrual cycles and corresponding hormonal shifts and—he argued—because men do not, "men are more like God than women."[9] This idea that not only is there something male about God but something God-like about men (and thus not about women) seems to shape, even if subconsciously, much of the critique against women in ministry. This is exactly what Mary Daly wrote in 1973, and here we are forty-five years later still dancing the same dance even when we proclaim a God that is beyond our understanding and experience of gender.[10]

---

8. This is the logical conclusion, that is, drawn by men in positions of power and authority who have a vested interest in remaining in positions of power and authority.

9. The biological and theological inaccuracy of his statement is clear. What is relevant, however, is that university students continue to hear this sort of thing—in the twenty-first century.

10. Daly (*Beyond God the Father*, 19ff) claims, "if God is male then the male is God" and then argues that patriarchy is a logical outcome of exclusively male language for God. Daly advocates for images of God that are both more theologically sound *and* liberative for women.

The Old Testament teaching that women are ungodlike and "ritually unclean" continued to shape the Christian tradition and was codified in the Roman Catholic Church in the year 1234 in *Corpus Iuris Canonici*. Because of their (our) ritual uncleanness women were prohibited from distributing communion, teaching in church, touching sacred objects including vestments, and even from singing in the congregational choir. And though within Catholicism parts of this law have been changed (women can, for example, teach and sing in the choir in Roman Catholic churches today), the notion that women are somehow or other unclean and can contaminate that which is holy has never completely disappeared from our cultural consciousness.

None of the women I interviewed were ever explicitly told they could not be pastors because of their menstrual cycles. However, several were told as children and teenagers that they were not allowed to be near the altar, because there was something about their girlness that made it inappropriate. One woman remembers being a very pious child and pleading to acolyte during confirmation. "This was in the early '70s, so Lutherans were ordaining women (only I didn't know it yet), but my pastor wouldn't let me. He said he didn't like seeing girls near the altar." And without women in positions of authority in the congregation, there was no one to argue her case for her, just a vague sense that being a girl made her unfit to serve the church in the same ways her equally adolescent and arguably more immature male peers were encouraged to. The message many of these women received was that their gender not only rendered them unable to pastor but that it also rendered them defective and unfit to be in close proximity, as one woman told me, "to sacred things."

## Objectification of Women's Bodies

Overwhelmingly the pastors I interviewed described the candidacy process as a positive experience. Most synods are doing a wonderful job most of the time with encouraging and supporting their female candidates during this time of discernment and formation.

As with most things, however, there were a few exceptions; one in particular in relationship to women and their bodies. One pastor told me, "Candidacy was a predominantly positive experience, but . . ." She went on to share that in one of her panel interviews, in which she was the only woman in the room, she was asked whether she had considered losing weight. She reflected that nothing in her candidacy essays or in previous conversations had suggested that her weight would be a topic of discussion. "It seemed to come out of nowhere and was very painful. If felt very objectifying. I wanted to respond, 'Oh, I'm fat? I didn't realize this. Thank you so much for letting me know.' But of course I didn't. He was a man in a position of power and I needed his 'approval'; I had given up everything to go to seminary. So, I don't remember what I said, only that I was humiliated." This person was not a lay member of the committee but a pastor. Pastors—especially male pastors—need to know that they have no right to talk about a woman's body like this. Period. She also wondered aloud to me whether or not any of her overweight male colleagues had been asked the same thing.

And yet comments about weight are common. Many women told about experiences of congregants commenting on their weight—whether it was weight gain or weight loss, whether it was perceived as a good thing ("Wow, Pastor, you look hot!") or a concern ("You don't look so good, Pastor. Are you sick?") Weight, hair style, clothing choices, makeup all seem to be fair game for critique. People seem to feel freer to offer "friendly" advice and to criticize the appearance of female pastors than male. Though female pastors receive such unsolicited advice and comments from both men and women, there seems to be a demographic difference in both the type and tenor of the comments. That is, women are more inclined to comment on style—"I love your dress!" or "Red toenails? Hmm . . ." Such comments are often too familiar, but they are rarely objectifying and never threatening. Comments from men, however, are more likely to contain sexual undertones or to be bullying.

Many women shared having been told at various points along their journey—beginning in candidacy—that their appearance, whether because they "are too pretty," "are too thin," or "wear too much makeup," will be a distraction to their male congregants. And such comments are often presented as if they are intended as a compliment: "I didn't know pastors could be so pretty." Or "I didn't know pastors were allowed to be sexy." Almost all of the women I interviewed have had men make inappropriately familiar comments that bordered on (or crossed the line completely to) sexual harassment. One woman, for example, had an older—and much larger—male parishioner wink and tell her, "I've half a mind just to take you home with me." The reverse also happens. Several pastors shared stories of parishioners objecting to them *because* of their bodies. Several of my interviewees have heard variations of "I can't take communion from someone with boobs."

Several women also shared experiences of having not only male parishioners but male colleagues accuse them of "using" their bodies. "I once had an older male colleague tell me that I had an unfair advantage because I could use my 'feminine presence' to win people. I don't think of myself as particularly feminine—not a big makeup, jewelry or fancy clothes sort, and not beautiful. So I was surprised he would even think this."

The fear that men will perceive women as trying to "use" their femininity inappropriately has shaped many female pastors. As one said, the implicit message we receive—especially from men, including our male colleagues, is, "Don't make me think of you as a woman. Make me think of you as a gender-neutral pastor." But "gender-neutral" is code for male—or at least for not female. And many female pastors have received this message from other women as well. One pastor told me that she recalls being told by a female preaching professor: "You do not want to do or wear any-thing to distract from the gospel. You want to be as plain as pos-sible." Her response was, "Well, that's bullshit . . . I want to present the gospel in a way that is authentic to who I am."

Male pastors are rarely, if ever, accused of "dressing too sexy," and yet many female pastors have been directly accused of this, and most worry about it. Much of the social policing of women's appearance comes from other women. Many pastors told me that they have had older women get upset because they wore red lipstick or nail polish or because they presided over the Eucharist with open-toed shoes. Here there seems to be something of a generational difference among female clergy. Several older pastors expressed frustration with younger female pastors they perceive as making it harder for women in ministry. "Especially in regards to clothing. Wear conservative, professional clothing. Conduct worship in close-toed shoes. Don't give folks ammunition with dress or makeup. Try to keep gender assumptions from interfering with doing ministry. You don't have to fight every battle."

## Embodiment and Vulnerability

One of the pastors I interviewed shared that she normally wears long pants in church, and during worship she wears an alb. One summer afternoon when she was not working, she ran into a member of her congregation out in the community. She was wearing shorts. Her parishioner, a woman of roughly the same age, exclaimed with a degree of both surprise and clearly with a sense of humor, "You have legs!" A number of pastors shared having heard comments about their bodies being lost in their albs or, when they removed their albs after worship, people expressing surprise that they "had" a body. Many such comments come with observations about the women's size, variations of: "You're so small." Such comments seem to highlight the vulnerability of the human body, particularly of the female human body.

Pregnant pastors carry an additional burden as they embody ministry. A pregnant body cannot be a nongendered or male body. One pastor shared having had a male member of her congregation comment late in her pregnancy, "Your belly finally sticks out further than your boobs do." Another pastor, pregnant with her third child, was asked by a male colleague, in a public setting, "Do you need me to explain how that happens?" For many congregants a pastor's pregnancy becomes a very difficult transition to navigate. In addition to all of the unsolicited and contradictory advice and the unwelcome touching that all pregnant women are subject to, female pastors have to address parishioners' concerns about maternity leave, and often they have to address personal or family decisions about finances and childcare in a very public way. One of the bishops I spoke with noted that it was not uncommon for the finance committee of any given congregation to begin asking about a female pastor cutting back to part time as soon as she makes it public that she is pregnant while when the wife of a male pastor gets pregnant, especially with the couple's first child, finance committees are often eager to suggest a raise to the church council so that the pastor can support his young, growing family. One pastor I interviewed told me that her church council, upon learning she was pregnant, was immediately concerned with her childcare arrangements: "What will you do if your child gets sick on Sunday?" This is a question they would have been very unlikely to ask a male pastor whose wife was pregnant.

Unsolicited advice and unstated assumptions about pregnancy and childrearing do not come only from parishioners. A number of women who were serving as associate pastor when they had a child shared stories of returning from maternity leave only to find that the male senior pastor had reappropriated certain pastoral duties because he felt a new mother would not be able to handle both motherhood and her full-time pastoral load. Another pastor said that when her first child had been born while she was in seminary, the seminary's director of contextual education told her she needed to postpone internship for a year because the baby was too young for her to go to work. Experiencing the presumption that others know what is best for the pastor's body and the pastor's family seems to be rather common.

Quite a few of the women I interviewed were very reflective about the nature of pregnancy and ministry. "When I was pregnant, I reached a point where it didn't feel safe for me to climb into our pulpit—it had narrow stairs and no railing. It wasn't a big deal, I preached from the chancel, but I was acutely aware that this space was not made for me. And yet, I am here." The sense that pregnancy highlighted the strangeness of women in ministry was a feeling shared by quite a few pastors. Even congregations that are quite open to women in ministry seem less sure what to do when those same women are pregnant.

A number of women found humor in their pregnancy experiences. One woman shared that she and her husband were copastoring when she was pregnant with her first child. They had gone out to eat one night and heard three men talking at another table, complaining about their pastors. "One man was complaining about his pastor's sermons, another about his pastor's lack of visits, and then a third—a voice we recognized—said, 'Y'all think you got troubles, my pastor's pregnant.'" She said that when she and her husband finished eating, they made sure to walk by the men, smile, and speak to them.

Beyond pregnancy, many pastors expressed feeling pulled by the demands of both family and ministry. "I know I disappoint people. Sometimes it is my family, because I'm too much at the church. And sometimes it's the church, because my family needs me." More than one woman expressed feeling as if they were always shortchanging either church or home. One pastor who is a member of a clergy couple said it this way: "We share everything at work. Everything. The preaching, the counseling, the visiting, the planning. And at home we share a lot of things—including cooking and cleaning. But we don't share helping the kids with their homework. Or sick kid care. Or Christmas shopping. God, I hate Christmas shopping." Relational domestic chores were—by far—the area that women expressed feeling the most "stuck" with: handling childcare or parent care, keeping track of doctor and dental appointments, managing all things school related, or tracking birthdays and other important dates for extended family members. The emotional work of being the key point person on all family relations, especially during the peak church-year times of Christmas and Easter, exhausts many female clergy.

Several women I interviewed expressed frustration at societal caregiving expectations placed on them: in addition to being expected to care for their own children and families, these pastors are expected to be better than their male colleagues at children's and youth ministry simply because of their gender. "I'm expected not only to like children but to be *good* with them because I'm a woman. But I'm not that good with them really. I'm learning, but it is not as natural as people assume it is supposed to be." The assumption that women should be better at doing ministry with children and youth has a correlated assumption that men are the more natural senior pastors. And this assumption has significant financial implications. Congregations resist paying pastors who specialize (or are perceived to specialize) in ministry with children and youth—a calling deemed to be less prestigious and important—on par with pastors perceived as the senior or "main" pastors—a calling deemed to be more important precisely because of the power and prestige that accompanies it. Many of the female pastors who are serving as associates with male senior pastors, *even when the male senior pastor is younger and less experienced*, expressed experiencing this expectation not only from the congregation, but from the senior pastor as well.

And yet for many women the children and youth *are* an integral part of their vocation, and they lift this up as part of the distinct gifts women can bring to the ministry. A number of women (and men as well) came into full-time pastoral ministry by way of youth and family ministry. One woman who had been a church preschool teacher and director of Christian education before discerning a call to seminary shared, "I think being a woman—and someone who was first a preschool teacher—helps me in ministry. It helps me to be a calm presence. I think I carry compassion in a way that is different from most of my male colleagues. It isn't that they aren't compassionate, but it is received differently."

Women *are* received differently from men. And this does not always work against them. One woman clearly delighted in telling me this story: "One time before worship as the assisting minister and I were robing, we heard a child in the sanctuary fussing. I said, 'Boy, I hope that's not my child.' He responded, "What do you mean? They're all yours.' And he was right. That's how I feel." Many of the women who expressed being most satisfied in their current congregational context expressed similar feelings of some degree of belonging to the congregation and of the members belonging to them. The same may very well be true for male pastors, but it is interesting to note that many female pastors did express this primarily in maternal, and thus traditionally feminine, terms.

Several women reported having been told at some point in their ministry that they needed to avoid expressing emotions; particularly they were told not to cry. One woman said this message began during her internship when her supervising pastor critiqued her sermons, suggesting she was sometimes too emotional. She took him seriously, listened to recordings of her sermons, and asked members of her internship committee to listen as well. She did not cry in any of the sermons, but noted that occasionally her voice would catch. "Every time it was at a point where I was speaking of God's grace." She notes that she has since witnessed a number of excellent male pastors who also express emotion in their preaching and that her supervisor's criticism was not representative of all male pastors or supervisors, but it made internship—and thus pastoral formation—more challenging. Another woman shared: "I do think I am more willing to be vulnerable, to cry, than many of my male colleagues. I often cry when the children's choir sings. I also cry at funerals, but I am aware that the family does not need me weeping. And for a long time I would apologize for my tears. But holy, sacred moments make me tear up. That is an authentic part of who I am. I don't worry so much about it anymore." Several women noted feeling that when or if they became emotional—whether in preaching or pastoral care— they were perceived as weak, but that when a male pastor becomes emotional in the very same moments he is perceived as tender, compassionate, or even holy.

## Sexual Misconduct: Women as "After-Pastors"

Everyone agrees that clergy sexual misconduct must be discussed, but not everyone agrees on how the church should respond to such misconduct. Clergy sexual misconduct cases almost always involve a male pastor and a female parishioner. In fact, I asked several of the bishops if they had ever had a sexual misconduct case involving a female pastor. They each acknowledged that such has probably happened, but they could not recall such an instance. Several of the bishops and assistants to bishops shared with me that they routinely send female pastors to serve as interims in congregations following the removal of a male pastor for sexual misconduct. One judicatory official explained, "After sexual misconduct cases, a female pastor has been able to help the congregation recognize that the misconduct was the fault of the pastor, not the female congregational member. This has helped folks see the power dynamics at play. He misused power and privilege and violated trust—she has helped them see that there is no way he is the victim." Inherent in this claim is the recognition of the complexity of gendered power dynamics, a complexity not always acknowledged in the church.[11]

Quite a few of the women I spoke with told their own stories of being the "after-pastor." In most cases they expressed very mixed feelings about it. They realized they were in something of a lose-lose situation. Congregations do not want to see their previous (often beloved) pastor as the "bad guy," and to enter a situation with power dynamics already so skewed rarely works in favor of the female pastor. She comes in with relatively less power (with less power than either the previous, male pastor or the church members angry about his removal). The judicatory officials who intentionally send female clergy in after sexual misconduct do so, in large part, because they recognize the cognitive dissonance created when a congregation is forced to face the contrasting cultural expectations. It is the pastoral office, not the gender of the person who occupies it, where the authority—and thus the responsibility for maintaining appropriate boundaries—lies. And yet, placing female pastors—pastors who are considerably more likely to, themselves, be recipients of unwanted sexual behavior (see chapter 5)—into a situation that is often emotionally charged along very gendered lines can set the female "after-pastor" and the congregation up for failure. One judicatory official, recognizing the

11. This is and other Boundaries Training issues are addressed further in Chapter 6.

potential problems with using female pastors immediately following a sexual misconduct, noted, "It is a question of safety. I'm not sure I'd want to just place a woman in a congregation after a sexual misconduct. Emotions are high. Anxiety is heightened. I won't put anyone in a dangerous situation. If this would be a hostile situation, it isn't worth the risk."

However, a few women know they were sent in as "after-pastors" precisely because it was the congregation who had requested it. After a sexual misconduct, sometimes congregations perceive a woman as both a safer and perhaps a more nurturing choice. One female judicatory official expressed the tension this way: "I really struggle with misconduct cases. It seems counterintuitive to send in a female pastor after a sexual misconduct because congregations almost always blame the woman. And yet, sometimes a woman in that role is the best way forward." A congregation's or bishop's decision, on the basis of gender perceptions, that a woman is inherently better suited than a man as an interim after sexual misconduct is, it seems, ill-advised. After pastoral sexual misconduct both congregations and interim pastors are uniquely vulnerable.

## Holy Ground Moments:

Though they recognized that such comments were stereotypes, each of the bishops stressed the church's need for both male and female leadership, precisely because pastoral ministry exercised by men and women is experienced differently. As one bishop said, "I want to avoid stereotypes; much of the perceived differences are socialized. But socialization is still real." Another bishop, speaking of the gifts he sees in female pastors, said, "I don't want to perpetuate stereotypes. But, female pastors often seem to excel at pastoral care; they more often get the importance of community."

In fact several of the bishops commented on the more collaborative nature of the female pastors they know. One bishop said:

> Male pastors are more likely to assume they can "preach"
> their way to a vision. I can go into a congregation and
> yank things around and if you don't like it, you can find

another church—bully-like—force my vision on a community. Male pastors often do this—and then when they leave, the vision collapses. Women can't do this. So they often work harder to build consensus, to build up the community; they have a greater need to win hearts than men do. So they do it. In the end, this helps the congregations they serve, they people the lead. They often create more enduring change perhaps because of the means they have at their disposal.

For these reasons, this bishop went on to say that female pastors tended to change the community in lasting ways in a way that, he said, "male leaders simply cannot."

Several of the bishops also commented on what they perceive to be a gap in quality of pastoral care. "Our female pastors do pastoral care differently—probably better overall—than male pastors, including me." And it is not just the bishops. The female pastors themselves perceive pastoral care as an area in which they are at an advantage over their male colleagues. One pastor noted, "I was talking to a male colleague about how many pastoral care visits he had made that week. The number was ridiculous. Like he must not have spent more than fifteen minutes with any one person. I visited less people. But I gave each person the gift of time." As she continued to talk with me about this, and about the various conversations she had had with male colleagues around time and attention expectations during pastoral care visits, I could not help wondering how such gendered assumptions about care become excuses that allow any male pastors who may feel uncomfortable in some pastoral care situations to minimize their own discomfort while a female pastor with the very same discomfort has no such "excuse."

One question I asked each of the female pastors I interviewed was whether there were any holy ground moments that they felt were made possible because they were women. The majority of answers to this question had to do with pastoral care opportunities—times when both men and women divulged to them stories of sexual violence, of domestic violence, or of childhood traumas—stories they may have hesitated to share with a male pastor.

Parishioners also told female pastors about medical situations—a miscarriage or the loss of a child, for example—that had never been shared before.

One pastor remembers sitting in the hospital waiting room with a male parishioner during his wife's surgery. After they had talked and prayed together, he said, "Pastor, I didn't vote for you. I could not imagine having a woman as a pastor. But you have changed my mind." Later she shared that he became much more vulnerable with her than she imagines he ever would have with a male pastor. Another pastor told of a time when she was doing baptismal counseling with a family. They had a newborn and a toddler. The toddler, pointing to the Lutheran Book of Worship, asked, "What is this?" I told her it was a hymnal. She thought about this for a moment and then wanted to know where the "hernal" was. "She taught me to question. To realize the way our words and actions might be perceived by a child. But I also realized that she saw me with a collar on having that conversation. Her world looks different because of this." Quite a few of the women noted that the recognition that they were a role model for the children and youth, especially the little girls, was one of the most humbling and holiest parts of their call. "I have one little girl in particular that follows me around all the time, helping with anything she can. I know she did not do that with the previous, male pastor. I didn't know if it is because I'm a woman, or if it just that the two of us 'click,' but it is certainly giving her a sense that she could be a pastor when she grows up."

Another woman responded by telling me that a Roman Catholic church had recently asked her to speak about being a woman in ministry.

> Part of what I said was that I feel a protection from the gospel when I preach. Because it isn't about me. It is about this amazing gift of grace. And as soon as I'm done preaching, I turn it over to God. I do feel good and confident in the pulpit. Many times I've had someone say to me, "I know you wrote that sermon just for me." And,

of course, I didn't. But this helps remind me that it isn't really me. This is about God.

Another woman echoed this: "The sacred work we do, the stuff you know about people's struggles, you look out from the pulpit and you can't dwell on that. But then they come up for communion and you give them grace. This can be overwhelming." And yet another pastor, a woman with nearly thirty years of ministry experience, expressed an acute awareness of both the beauty and the heartbreak of ministry: "Mostly I think about this whole life as a privilege. It's not about gender, it's about the work of clergy, about holy ground times. Some of the moments which often seem most sacred are the most routine—when people are sick and dying. I know God is with us in these tender moments. This life is a sacred trust."

And sometimes the holy ground comes in the form of manual labor. One pastor serving a small, rural congregation in a community where one might expect her to struggle as a female religious leader told me the following story:

> We were doing some repair/remodeling work in the sanctuary and the altar was being refinished by an elderly man in the congregation who did woodworking as a hobby. We had talked about the work, what the council had recommended. But when he called me to come see the finished piece and I walked into the sanctuary I was taken aback by what he had done. I walked behind the altar and stood for a moment before making eye contact with him. The altar was perfect! And it was a good eight or nine inches lower than it had been. He smiled at me and said, "Not all pastors are over six feet tall."

## Suggested Resources

DeConick, April D. *Holy Misogyny: Why the Sex and Gender Conflicts in the Early Church Still Matter.* New York: Continuum, 2011.

Manne, Kate. *Down Girl: The Logic of Misogyny.* New York: Oxford University Press, 2018.

Wolf, Naomi. *The Beauty Myth: How Images of Beauty Are Used against Women.* New York: HarperCollins, 2002.

## Discussion Questions

1. What cultural gendered stereotypes (around toys, rules, chores, and so forth) did you grow up with? How have they shaped your adult life and expectations of gender?

2. Have you ever experienced being seen as a representative for a larger group, such as all women or all members of a particular ethnic group? How does that feel?

3. How does the objectification of women's bodies shape our interactions in our churches and communities?

4. Does expressing emotions at work—whether in leading worship or in other professional capacities—make one less professional or less proficient?

5. Do you think that men and women generally lead differently? If so, how? What are the strengths of each?

# 4

# Gatekeeping

In the movie *Monty Python and the Holy Grail*, King Arthur, Sir Robin, Sir Galahad, Sir Lancelot and another knight approach the Bridge of Death. Through the dense fog they see the Bridgekeeper from a distance. Arthur, with help from Sir Galahad, tells the others that the job of the Keeper of the Bridge of Death is to ask each traveler three questions. And, he continues, "anyone who answers all three questions correctly will be allowed to safely cross the bridge." Sir Robin asks, "What if you get a question wrong?" Arthur responds, "Then you are cast into the Gorge of Eternal Peril." The knights, in no hurry to be cast into the gorge, argue over who is to go first. Lancelot wins.

> "Stop! Who would cross the Bridge of Death must answer me these questions three, ere the other side he see."
>
> "Ask me the questions, Bridgekeeper. I am not afraid."
>
> "What is your name?
>
> "My name is Sir Lancelot of Camelot."
>
> "What is your quest?"
>
> "To seek the Holy Grail."
>
> "What is your favorite color?
>
> "Blue."
>
> "Right. Off you go."

The ease with which Sir Lancelot crosses the bridge emboldens the others. So Sir Robin immediately presents himself to the Bridgekeeper. Robin is also asked his name and his quest. But rather than his favorite color Sir Robin is asked, "What is the capital of Assyria?" When he responds indignantly, "I don't know that!" He is launched, screaming, into the Gorge of Eternal Peril. Sir Galahad approaches more cautiously, is asked the easier favorite color question, but stumbles answering and is, likewise, launched into the Gorge.

When King Arthur approaches the bridge, the third question he is asked is, "What is the air-speed velocity of an unladen swallow?" "What do you mean? An African or European swallow?" he asks the Bridgekeeper. "What?! I don't know that!" responds the Bridgekeeper and the Bridgekeeper is immediately launched into the Gorge of Eternal Peril. The remaining knight and King Arthur then cross the bridge with King Arthur saying, "Well, you have to know these things when you're a king, you know."[1]

## Gatekeeping as Explicit and Implicit Control

This scene provides an entertaining image of gatekeeping. Gatekeeping is about control and access. Often it is access to particular goods or services, but it can also be access to particular roles or privileges. In *Monty Python and the Holy Grail* the Bridgekeeper has control over access to a path—a literal, physical thing (a bridge) that serves as a metaphor of controlled access to a life's path. This thing over which the Bridgekeeper has access is *not* inherently his; it is something external to him. Thus there is a degree of power wielded by the Bridgekeeper, a power that can be exploited for his own amusement. But it is not an unlimited power, as the Bridgekeeper himself is also subject to the external forces for which or whom he acts as a gatekeeper.

1. Gillam and Jones, dirs., *Monty Python*.

Gatekeeping as a form of power is often a necessary good.[2] Many professions have gatekeepers. You cannot just choose to be a doctor, lawyer, pharmacist, professor, or pastor. An external, institutional entity (that almost always consists of those who have already attained the status for which they are gatekeeping) is responsible for determining the standards that are to be met and upheld. And we *want* gatekeepers! When my mom needed heart surgery, I was grateful for the gatekeeping of the medical profession. And when, as director of a youth and family ministry program, I place student interns in congregations under the supervision of a pastor, I am trusting in the gatekeeping of a variety of denominational bodies.

One of the crucial roles of gatekeeping is that of dues collection. That is, there is always a cost of some sort for access to whatever good gatekeeping is intended to protect. For many professions these dues include years of training and formation as well as a willingness to submit to a particular set of practices and standards. Therefore, institutionalized gatekeeping acts to protect the broader public; it serves the common good. Most denominations, for example, in addition to the gatekeeping of the academic work of seminary require extensive psychological tests of ministry candidates. This particular gatekeeping practice is intended to protect the church from someone who might desire a position of public ministry—and the power and authority that comes with it—for the wrong reasons. Gatekeeping functions to protect those who might be vulnerable to this power and authority.

Gatekeeping does not only happen on an institutional level but on an individual one as well. Sometimes individual gatekeeping is integral to a larger institutional structure. For example, within the university structure where I work, there is a clear hierarchy: faculty report to school chairs, and school chairs to college deans, and college deans to the university provost. The individuals who occupy the positions of chair, dean, and provost all play

2. Thanks to my colleague Dr. Beth Wright, professor of sociology, for helping me clarify the application of gatekeeping to the enforcement of cultural religious norms.

gatekeeping roles for those below them in the university structure. Information critical to professional success is often disseminated through these channels.

When such gatekeeping works as intended, the institution works more efficiently. However, power can be misused. So, imagine a situation in which a school chair uses the position to control information and goods such that a desired, prestigious committee appointment or a speaking engagement or the most sought-after course in the program or a favorable teaching time slot is offered only to a faculty member in good standing with the chair, based on purely personal preference rather than on qualifications. The faculty member who receives this privileged access now has a fee of sorts to pay, such as deference, respect, or loyalty to the chair in future faculty disagreements, for example.

Though such a situation may be inappropriate, it is not illegal. Much unsanctioned gatekeeping, on the other hand, is illegal. Think, for example, of corrupt police officers, insider trading, and so on. And though it is illegal, and thus does not receive explicit institutional support, unsanctioned gatekeeping is often implicitly propped up by those in power or by larger cultural practices that reward rather than punish vigilante gatekeeping—or both. Unsanctioned gatekeepers possess a sense of both entitlement to and responsibility for guarding access to particular goods and services or rights and responsibilities usually for the (perceived) good of the sanctioned gatekeeper.

## What's in a Name?

One common form of gatekeeping is naming. Naming is an exercise of power. By naming something, the namer has not so much described or summarized the named as they have, in a concrete sense, *created* it. The namer has a particular perspective in relation to the named, and the process of actualizing that particular perspective—by creating the named in the perspective of the namer—limits the named in that they are now *unable* to act in a way that the namer does not sanction. Or, at least, when the namer is in a privileged position of power over the named, the named are unable to act without fear of repercussions. When the named acts in a way that displeases the namer, the namer is likely to change the name—often to reflect disapproval—allowing the cycle to repeat itself indefinitely. Plates become chipped plates, friends become best friends or former friends, and so on. In this way, the very act of naming creates a distinct power difference between the namer and the named.[3]

Considerable exegetical work has been done on this topic in regard to the naming of Eve by Adam (Gen 2:23). Some scholars insist that the act of naming is itself an act of power that contains within it the potential for domination. In giving Adam the power to name Eve, in other words, God gives Adam power over Eve. Others, however, suggest that the power to name is more rightly understood as an act of discernment. In other words, to name something (or someone) is not inherently an act of domination, but can be an act of description. The politics of this, however, are complex, as questions of power cannot be extracted from the practice of applying descriptions that are presumed to be normative.

Naming is not exclusively about creative power, but can also be a source of destructive power. The use of pejorative names (name-calling), which dehumanize, thus making another "other," often both precedes and accompanies violence whether that be the violence of war, domestic violence, or schoolyard bullying. In fact one might argue that it is precisely the power to name or discern the other as other that makes violence possible and renders the victims invisible.

Nearly every female pastor interviewed noted that they are often referred to with a gendered qualifier: "lady pastor," "female pastor," and even "pastorette." The use of qualifiers suggests that women are perceived as exceptions; insofar as we feel linguistically obligated to include gender (or race) in naming another we are making the implicit claim that male (and white) are normative. The qualifier may not, in fact, be an intended act of gatekeeping;

---

3. I owe this paragraph to a project I worked on with my son, Jordan Makant. In fact, he may well have been its original primary author.

but it does, at the very least, reflect internalized cultural norms that suggest that for a woman to be a pastor is an exception to the rule, an oddity worthy of note.[4]

One pastor with nearly thirty years of ministry experience and now serving in her fourth call says that the transition follows a predictable pattern. When first called to a new congregation she is always referred to and introduced as "our new lady pastor." As the congregation becomes comfortable with her and the newness wears off, she becomes "our lady pastor." And then as the novelty of having a female pastor wears off, she gradually becomes just "our pastor." (This pastor has always been the first woman to serve in the congregations to which she has been called and often has been the only woman in public ministry in the community, so, she noted, the evolution from "our lady pastor" to "our pastor" can take a while.) Once she has become "our pastor," this is the point at which she says she knows she is now fully accepted in her role. She sees this as a necessary evolution in the hearts and minds of a congregation and insists that in none of the congregations she has served did she perceive this as demeaning. Nonetheless, she also expressed feeling a sense of relief when the majority of a congregation had made the shift to "our pastor," because "now we're finally ready to do ministry together."

Sometimes, however, the qualifier is more clearly intended as disapproval. One pastor, who is the dean of her conference, relayed a story shared with her by a local male colleague. When the installation service for the new male colleague was being planned, the chair of the male pastor's call committee referred to the conference dean—who would be presiding over the installation—as "that lady pastor down the road." The female pastor shared this with me, saying, "I'm not sure how he meant it. But it felt demeaning. And his congregation had recently voted that they would *not* consider a female pastor." Additionally a member of the congregation she was serving had left and joined this other congregation when she was

---

4. We do the exact same thing with race, often indicating, for example, that the attorney, physician, teacher, and so forth is black or Latino but rarely, if ever, qualifying such a title by describing someone as white.

called, precisely because he did not want to be in a church with a "lady pastor." She went on to say, "It felt very awkward to be presiding at the installation. It was awkward—probably for both of us—to be together in that particular setting, with me in this role."

During my interviews with bishops and bishops' staffs one judicatory official told me that older men in particular are often very patronizing, calling female clergy "darling" and "sweetheart" or commenting on their appearance, especially their age or their size. Though most often such comments are *not* intended to be harassment and are not necessarily sexual in any way, they are definitely inappropriate—things the same men would be mortified to hear directed at a male pastor. One pastor shared with her bishop's office the story of an older man who was with her in the sacristy as they both robed for worship (he was a layperson serving as an assisting minister). He watched her robe and then said, "You're just so little; you disappear in a robe. It swallows you." The pastor did not assume malice on the man's part. Though she is a fairly average-sized women, he was, she imagined, genuinely surprised by her lack of stature compared to that of the previous, much larger male pastor who had served the congregation. But such statements belie assumptions of gender and power and authority even when they are not intended to be belittling or demeaning.

Such comments seem to be most prevalent when the female pastor is considerably younger than the male parishioner, particularly if the parishioner has grown children, or even grandchildren, the same age as the pastor. So the older male experiences what he is saying as expressing endearment. But regardless of the kindness with which his words are intended, the women interviewed almost always express feeling that such terms of endearment are a refusal to accept the pastor's authority *as* pastor. One pastor shares, "One of my greatest challenges is that I'm not only female, but that I look young. People treat me like I'm a child. I've even had one older man who continually patted me on the head. And there was another who always winked at me during the Eucharist. *When I served him the bread!* They treat me like I'm their child or even their grandchild, which, I think, really disrespects the office." Another pastor similarly tells of a male parishioner who not only insisted on calling her honey but also continually came up behind her to rub her shoulders. "I don't think he meant to be creepy; but it was inappropriate, and I should not have to keep saying that to someone."

When this came up in an interview with one of the judicatory officials, the official said that this was not an issue restricted to clergy/parishioner relationships but that it also came up with some regularity when a congregation had a middle-aged senior male pastor and a female associate pastor fifteen or more years his junior. The official shared a story of having had one senior pastor who insisted upon calling the female associate hon, honey, or sweetie even when she protested. She explained to both the senior pastor and later to a member of the bishop's staff that his continued use of such language in public settings undermined her pastoral authority and presence with members of the congregation. And then, the final straw for the female associate (who left the congregation shortly after this) was when she returned to work after maternity leave and the senior pastor informed her that he had decided—without consulting her first—that he was decreasing her preaching from twice a month to once a month, "because you're going to have less time now."

To give this pastor the benefit of the doubt, he may very well have been trying to be helpful. Men who have grown up assuming a degree of power and have certain perceptions of women and gender roles may believe such paternalism to be an appropriate form of caregiving. But it is a form of gatekeeping, a clear message—no matter how kindly it is put—that one cannot rightly be both a good full-time mother and a good full-time pastor. This is a message the same senior pastor would never have sent to a male associate pastor who had recently become a father.

Another pastor who serves as an associate pastor working with a male senior pastor a generation older tells of discussing her academic work with her colleague one day. She is currently working on a Doctor of Ministry (DMin) and the senior pastor neither has nor desires a doctoral degree. The senior pastor, upon realizing that she would soon finish the program, told her, "I hope you know that I'm *not* going to call you 'Doctor.'" She replied, "Well, that's okay. You don't call me 'Pastor' now." When I asked her what the senior pastor does call her in congregational or professional settings she said, "Always just my first name. But if I called him by his first name with other folks around, he'd be furious."

In settings such as these, the male senior pastor has the power to shape the way the entire congregation will respond to the associate pastor. One woman described the senior pastor she worked with as male, a generation-plus older, and significantly larger than she. He routinely refers to her as "young lady" or "kiddo" in front of the parishioners, including during worship. One older female parishioner who has been offended by this on behalf of the associate pastor counseled her to "lean in." But the pastor says she now realizes she cannot remain in this call and ever develop any pastoral authority as the senior pastor will simply not make space for it. The pattern is established. Many male senior pastors appear to see their female junior colleagues not as colleagues with whom to do ministry but as interns to train and mentor.

This power to use nicknames and to withhold or insist on the use of titles is a form of gatekeeping that is often quite subtle. Perhaps a story from a woman who is part of a clergy couple will make this even clearer. This clergy couple has always served together in the same congregation as copastors. They are roughly the same age (in their early sixties). Both went to seminary as second-career students with advanced degrees and experience in their previous occupations, and they graduated from seminary together, so they have equal years of ministry experience And yet this couple reports that when they are greeted—by parishioners and by members of the community—the male pastor is almost always referred to by title (Pastor) and last name whereas the female pastor is most often called simply by her first name. This happens whether they are separate or together. Additionally, the couple shared that after worship they have noticed that the male pastor is often told, "Great sermon, Pastor" whereas the female pastor is much more likely to hear "Nice talk," followed by her first name. And this continues to happen even though the husband has routinely tried to gently remind people "we are *both* Pastor (last name)."

Another pastor tells of having been repeatedly called honey by an older male member of the church council during council meetings. The pastor gently corrected him, saying, "My name is Pastor So-and-so," and "You can call me Pastor," and even "Please call me Pastor, not honey." The pastor finally said something to her male colleague—the senior pastor of the congregation, who was present during these exchanges. She told him, "You *need* to say something. It is past time for you to intervene." The male pastor expressed surprise, both that the female pastor had been bothered by the male parishioner, and even more that she held him responsible as well. He had neither noticed these exchanges nor considered intervening. She said that at first he thought she was creating an issue where none existed but that once this pattern was pointed out to him, he realized how prevalent it was, and he consistently intervened from then on—and slowly the atmosphere changed.

Such stories demonstrate just how crucial male colleagues can be as allies to women in ministry. Another woman, who now serves in a judicatory role, tells of working on a synodwide service project with a male pastor. The male pastor had coordinated the event and invited her to participate. She arrived at the site before he did and introduced herself to one of the workers, one who seemed to be in charge. She introduced herself as Pastor X. A few minutes later she overheard the man she had just introduced herself to asking someone else, "Who *is* that woman?" Shortly after this her male colleague arrived. He began introducing the female pastor to others at the site. The first introduction was to the man she had already met and who had just referred to her as "that woman." The male pastor said, "Let me introduce you to Pastor X. She is my friend and colleague. Well, actually she's my boss." The man's face, the female pastor told me, "was beautifully puzzled and embarrassed."

## Public Gatekeepers

A common form of public, institutional gatekeeping that many female clergy experience occurs in their work with ecumenical partners. In fact quite a few pastors identify ecumenical work as the most difficult work they do as female pastors. One pastor, who was serving as her bishop's ecumenical officer (and thus sometimes represented the bishop at ecumenical meetings) was attending a gathering that had been organized by one of the Roman Catholic dioceses with which her synod had close relations.

> It was like going back in time thirty years. It was awful. All of the bishops and representatives from a variety of churches—Protestant and Roman Catholic—were participating in worship leadership. We were having a planning meeting; the highlight of the service was to be a blessing of the participants by various clergy members. Folks were scrambling to make sure I wouldn't bless anyone. It was awkward because I was to be the only pastor *not* blessing anyone. This was clearly because I was a woman, not because I was Protestant. One older priest actually stood up in the middle of this conversation, pointed to three nuns and said, 'They have been doing your pastoral care. You should respect them.' He then turned back to me and said, 'And we should respect her.' But I was not allowed to participate in the blessing. I told my bishop I would never go back. I was not putting myself in that position again.

Several pastors shared stories of the challenges associated with ecumenical weddings. A wedding between a Lutheran and a Roman Catholic took place in the Catholic church with the priest presiding. The female Lutheran pastor (and the pastor of the husband) was invited both to preach and to bless the rings. When she arrived at the church for the service, the priest would not allow her to sit in the chancel—it was too near the altar—but insisted she sit in the pew with the groom's family. The bride's mother, an active member of the Catholic church, was mortified.

Another pastor told of having been invited to co-officiate the wedding of a member of her congregation. The young woman had grown up in the congregation, and she and the pastor had a very close relationship. The couple completed all of their premarital counseling with the female Lutheran pastor, and yet when the time for the wedding itself came, the groom's family objected so strongly to the idea of a "woman pastor that I had to step down and hand over the wedding to someone with the right anatomical parts even though he did not know or love the couple."

Many women told stories of having been intentionally excluded from the local ecumenical (and all-male) clergy groups. One pastor told of serving in a community where the local group would not even include her when they were planning a domestic violence awareness prayer vigil—and she regularly worked with a local domestic violence response organization! Moreover, the members of the all-male clergy group, with what I am sure was unintentional irony, called the event Ending the Silence. Unfortunately, even when women are included in predominantly male ecumenical groups, they often do not feel that are being welcomed as equals. One woman said the first time she showed up for a meeting of one all-male clergy group, she was immediately "invited" to be the group's secretary—an honor she politely declined.

For the majority of women, however, the greatest challenges to their "right" to ordination comes not from within the congregation they serve and not from other ecumenical work but from complete strangers in public settings. One of the things that I found most surprising in this study was the sheer number of female pastors who have experienced resistance bordering on harassment (and in some cases even assault) in hospital settings. Nearly 25 percent of the women interviewed shared stories of gatekeeping in hospital settings. Some of these are mild incidents—more incidents of disbelief than of intentional maltreatment. Many women told about running into someone in a hospital who upon noticing the collar, asked questions such as "What are you?" "You can't be a priest, can you?" "Do people call you Father?" "Are you a nun?" When they are grounded in a genuine lack of knowledge that women can be pastors, these questions become for many women opportunities for conversation about ministry, Scripture interpretation, and faithfulness in following God's call in one's life.

But many times the questions are not innocent, and they are not grounded in a lack of knowledge or imagination but are instead challenges to the pastor's authority and right to exercise the office of pastor.[5] One pastor shared a story of visiting a parishioner in a large inner-city hospital. She was wearing a collar *and* she had a clergy badge for the hospital she was visiting. When she pulled into the parking lot and turned towards the designated clergy parking area she was stopped by a parking lot attendant and told she couldn't park there, that area was reserved for pastors. When she told the attendant that she *was* a pastor and showed him her badge, he shook his head and repeated that she could not park there. She notes, "It was as if there were a willful refusal to even hear the words I was saying. Something in him simply could not or would not allow the words to sink in."

Another pastor shared a story of going to the hospital to visit a member of her congregation while she was pregnant. "I was wearing a cleric [clerical collar]. I was stopped by a member of the hospital staff at the desk as I walked in. And I was quizzed. She did not believe I was really a pastor. She insisted on seeing credentials because she had never seen a pregnant pastor before. I was furious about being delayed, but I was also frustrated that this was coming from a woman." Most of the struggles faced by female pastors in hospitals are experienced as frustrations because the women describe being so focused on the task at hand and concerned about the welfare of the person they are visiting that they are caught totally off guard by the challenge.

But occasionally the challenges have been more directly hostile. One pastor shared a story of going to visit an elderly parishioner who was in ICU and not expected to live much longer.

5. Experiences of physical intimidation and sexual violence are addressed more fully in Chapter 5. As a reminder, thirteen of the eighty-five pastors interviewed shared stories of violence or threats of violence. This suggests that slightly more than one-quarter of female pastors experience physical threats simply for being female pastors.

I was just hoping to get there in time to pray with him before he died. I was wearing my collar, walking into the hospital, and lost in my thoughts about the situation I was walking into. I realized there was a man walking out of the hospital who was walking towards me. I stepped to my side, looked up, and said, 'Excuse me.' He stepped in front of me, making it clear (which it probably should have already been) that he intended to block my path. That is when I really realized that he was a large man, much larger than me and he was not going to just let me walk in. I looked at him again and said, "Excuse me, please. I need to see someone." He continued blocking my path and said, "And what gives *you* the right to wear that collar?" I mean, I was in the midst of doing ministry—not thinking about my gender—and then you have to defend who you are and what you're doing.

She said that she finally got past him but had been so shaken by the encounter that she went to the bathroom and cried. She then remembered the man in ICU, collected herself, and went to his bedside to be pastor and priest. I asked if she had ever shared this experience with anyone—with her colleagues or her bishop. And she said no. It had scared her and made her angry. But it had also seemed something to be ashamed of, so she had not shared it.

Sometimes the implied threat to women in ministry is not of potential physical or sexual violence from the questioner, but of damnation, of punishment from God. One pastor who is an outspoken advocate for social justice was interviewed on television. Shortly after her interview she received the following handwritten note:

Dear Miss [First Name]:

I saw you on TV and noticed you had a collar around your neck. Are you a Bishop or a member of the clergy?

Have you read 1st Timothy, chapter 3, verses 1–5? (King James of course) I don't believe you qualify for any office of the clergy.

I am concerned about your soul. Let me ask you this question. Do you know Jesus? I don't mean in your head, but in your heart. There is a sad difference.

Have you ever realized you are a sinner? <u>Romans 3:23</u>: For all have sinned, and come short of the glory of God.

Have you ever ask Jesus to forgive you of your sin? <u>Romans 6:23</u>: For the wages of sin is death; but the gift of God is eternal life through Jesus Christ our Lord. Last, but not least: <u>Romans 10:13</u>: For whosoever shall call upon the name of the Lord shall be saved.

I pray you have done this. No one has to go hell. No one!

I have enclosed a gospel tract for you to read. Please do so.

Sincerely: Someone who is concerned about your soul![6]

Everything about this letter is an act of gatekeeping; and the gatekeeper presumes to be speaking on behalf of God. Note first that the author refers to the pastor, a complete stranger, as "Miss" and then uses her first name. And if the refusal to use an appropriate title were insufficient to make the point, the author goes on to say that the pastor does not qualify for the office based on the supposed evidence of Scripture. The Pauline and deutero-Pauline prohibitions against women in positions of authority over men and Paul's admonition that women are to remain silent in church are in practice the predominant arguments against women in ministry. These are certainly the "fights" female pastors in the South most often face.[7]

Though this is not the place to adequately unpack the hermeneutical issues at play in interpreting the various texts that seem to limit appropriate roles of authority for women, it is important to name that underneath most of the resistance to women as pastors is

6. With permission of the recipient of this letter, a copy of it is included in the Appendix.

7. It should be noted that whereas the Evangelical Protestant resistance to women in ministry is solely a matter of Scripture interpretation (especially 1 Timothy) the Roman Catholic Church's prohibition against female priests is an argument of sacramental theology as much as it is interpretation of Paul. Gatekeepers who rely on either argument, however, are generally unable or unwilling to consider the possibility that another faithful interpretive lens exists, making these exceedingly frustrating encounters for many pastors.

a broader discomfort with women in positions of authority. Hermeneutics becomes weaponized for sociocultural, not theological, reasons.[8] And it is important to acknowledge that in many areas of our country (and world) these undercurrents are becoming stronger rather than weaker. Thus, such experiences for female pastors and public leaders are more frequent than one might be wont to believe. One woman I interviewed, a pastor who is also well known and respected as a scholar, has been asked, "How can you do what you do and say you believe in the Bible?" Another woman, when asked, "So, really, you're a lady preacher?" was then told, "Well, at my church we actually follow the Bible. And that means women remain silent in church." And—it should be noted—this remark came from a woman. Another pastor shared that when she was doing Clinical Pastoral Education (CPE) during seminary, she was one of only two women at her site. The other members were all men (one of them was also an ELCA student). One male student from a denomination that does not ordain women expressed discomfort even with participating in a CPE group with women. Perhaps to appeal to him, the male ELCA colleague agreed that he had "doubts" about women in ministry, and the only other woman, the spouse of a Southern Baptist pastor, quickly offered, "I'm doing CPE so I can be a better pastor's wife when I go on hospital visits." No one in the group defended the female seminarian's right even to participate in CPE, let alone to be a candidate for ministry.

Such interactions do not occur in a cultural vacuum. John Piper is a well-known Evangelical pastor and teacher. He produces a regular podcast called *Ask Pastor John*, in which he answers questions of theology, Scripture interpretation, and church practices. I mention three such podcast episodes from the past few years, not because Piper is a good theologian (he is not), but because he has a large following especially among younger Evangelicals, and because he offers "clear biblical principles" that he presents as beyond argument. In his podcast from February 16, 2015, Piper asks the question, "Can a Woman Preach if Elders Affirm it?"[9] The

8. Chapter 6 addresses biblical hermeneutics.

9. Piper, "Can a Woman Preach." Piper's multifaceted ministry is called

affirming elders would, necessarily, be men. Piper, using 1 Tim 2:11–14 argues based on the order of creation (Adam then Eve) and a gendered tendency to corruptibility (Eve was deceived by Satan, not Adam) that preaching (and the authority to preach) is not about competence (yes, he actually says this) but about roles—and women are not to play any role in which they exercise authority over men. Several months later Piper asks the seemingly unrelated question, "Should women be police officers?"[10] His answer is an interesting mental gymnastics routine: A woman *may* choose to be city planner who has indirect authority over men (for example, she may decide where stop signs are placed) but may not faithfully choose to be a police officer because if she, as a woman, were directing traffic (and thus cars, many presumably driven by men), this would violate the God-given relationship between men and women. It is, he makes clear, the direct interaction that makes female authority unbiblical. And lest one think 2015 was just a particularly bad year for Piper, on January 22, 2018, Piper asks the question, "Is there a place for female professors at seminary?"[11] Piper's answer is, of course, no. Why? Because by college, boys are men and no longer in the gray area of adolescence; and as they are training for public ministry (something for which women are unfit by virtue of their gender), allowing women to teach ministry-related courses would be theologically inconsistent. Again, women are unfit to teach in seminaries not because they lack the intellectual ability or skill, but because Piper's understanding of the right relationship between men and women would be compromised by the very nature of an interaction between an adult female teacher and an adult male student.

Piper is not alone. As I'm writing this a group of (male) Evangelical pastors has released a statement condemning social justice as antithetical to the Christian faith. As of this writing, over 6,600 Evangelicals have signed this statement. The statement argues that social justice is an inherent part of a secular culture that is

Desiring God. This is episode 533 of his podcast *Ask Pastor John*.

10. Piper, "Should Women Be Police Officers?"

11. Piper, "Is There a Place."

"currently undermining Scripture in the areas of race and ethnicity, manhood and womanhood, and human sexuality."[12] And though much that might be said regarding this statement, the culture it reflects, and the power that it wields, the section that is directly relevant to women in ministry is Section XI, "Complementarianism."

> We affirm that God created mankind both male and female with inherent biological and personal distinctions between them and that these created differences are good, proper, and beautiful. Though there is no difference between men and women before God's law or as recipients of his saving grace, we affirm that God has designed men and women with distinct traits and to fulfill distinct roles. These differences are most clearly defined in marriage and the church, but are not irrelevant in other spheres of life. In marriage the husband is to lead, love, and safeguard his wife and the wife is to respect and be submissive to her husband in all things lawful. In the church, qualified men alone are to lead as pastors/elders/bishops and preach to and teach the whole congregation. We further affirm that the image of God is expressed most fully and beautifully in human society when men and women walk in obedience to their God-ordained roles and serve according to their God-given gifts.

None of this is new. As one of the pastors I spoke with said, she tells her male colleague whenever such comments are made in public, "#justanotherday." Pastors who are publicly outspoken seem to face more direct resistance than those who are quieter or less public. The pastor who received the letter trying to save her from hell told me, "I have no internal conflict between femininity and a strong pastoral identity, but publicly this is too often seen as incompatible." This refusal to adhere to widely accepted gender norms triggers public forms of gatekeeping. Women who challenge traditional notions of gender become, in a substantive way, gate crashers who represent a threat to what is perceived as a necessary stability of the status quo. As one of my male academic colleagues has often said regarding academia, "Stasis is good." Stasis means

12. See [MacArthur et al.,] *Statement.*

that nothing changes. That power remains unchallenged. So, stasis is only good for those who benefit from the current power structures. Women in ministry, by virtue of their very existence, challenge a clear cultural stasis. And this challenge makes many people very uncomfortable.

Thus, many female pastors report that they are not the only ones challenged by public gatekeepers; often their congregations and families are as well. Several pastors shared that when members of their community who are not part of their congregation learn they are pastors, these community members immediately ask who the "senior" pastor is. There is often an assumption that it is—maybe—acceptable for a congregation to employ a female pastor as long as there is a real pastor (who is definitionally male) in charge. Similarly many interviewed pastors shared that one of their greatest challenges in the community and in the early stages of congregational life is for and with their spouse. "People want to know what my husband's role is. They don't have a frame of reference for a pastor's husband." And this is multiplied exponentially for partnered lesbian pastors.

## Bishops: Institutional Gatekeepers

Bishops serve as institutionally authorized gatekeepers. Many—most, in fact—of the pastors I interviewed express tremendous love for their bishops. And the great majority share feeling completely supported by their bishops. However, due to the intimate nature of the relationship a pastor may have, or at least hope to have, with her bishop, pastors who have experienced resistance or even outright scorn or rejection from their bishops on account of their gender describe this as among the most painful and debilitating of gatekeeping experiences.

One pastor shares of having been "at a conference meeting where I was the only woman present. The bishop at the time spent probably twenty minutes ranting about how the ministry of women were [sic] destroying the church. And only one of my male colleagues challenged him." This was in the late 1980s and that particular individual is no longer an active bishop. But a few pastors continue to experience resistance from bishops today. One pastor tells of having been among a group of female pastors who approached their bishop to request that a female pastor—not necessarily a member of the group making the request—be invited to preach for the upcoming synod assembly in the year of the fortieth anniversary of women's ordination. The bishop reportedly responded that "A woman will *never* preach at synod assembly." When I asked the female pastor if this was a clear policy or practice, she said that a woman had never preached at any synod event in that synod.[13] This pastor is not alone in having left a synod because she became too discouraged and even exhausted from a continued lack of support of, and at times direct resistance to, her ministry from the bishop.

Pastors *and* bishops commented on the importance of bishops' support for women to be successful in ministry. On the one hand, several people noted that part of why the synod they serve was so far "behind" in terms of women in ministry (and this comment came from people in more than one synod) is because of the antagonism from preivous bishops toward women in ministry. In some cases previous bishops actively worked against women in ministry in "their" synods and in some cases the bishops were more passive, neglecting the needs of the women in their synods.

On the other hand, many pastors describe their bishop as their greatest ally. Several report taking great comfort in knowing that they feel invited and safe sharing their struggles in ministry with their bishop. One of the things that surprised me—though perhaps it should not have—is that the bishops female clergy seemed to most appreciate were also the bishops least likely to themselves recognize that they were doing anything particularly helpful for the female pastors. One of the clearest examples of this surrounds public synodical worship practices. Several bishops made it clear

13. It should be noted that (a) the bishop who allegedly made this remark is now retired, and (b) he was not bishop of any of the synods of this study. This interaction with that bishop was the determining factor in the pastor leaving that synod.

that though they do not often say anything about the importance of women in ministry, it is simply a matter of practice that at any synod worship service, if a man preaches, a woman presides; and if a man presides, a woman preaches.

Acts of judicatory gatekeeping that gently but firmly insist on the equality of the ministry of women and men are crucial to the long-term vitality of women's ministry and to the health of the church. Implicit messages have a greater formational practice than explicit ones, precisely because they are received subconsciously such that we do not choose to accept or reject them. So, for example, were a bishop to publicly state at a synod assembly that the preacher at the closing worship will rotate every year—female one year, male the next—this would be unlikely to shape the imaginations of the participants in worship in any substantive way. However, that all who attend assembly in a synod where women routinely participate in leadership experiences either a female presider or preacher means that all who attend synod assembly can now indeed imagine a female pastor because they have seen, heard, and experienced one in action, even if they do not later remember why they believe that women can indeed make excellent pastors.

## Suggested Resources

Grenz, Stanley, with Denise Muir Kjesbo. *Women in the Church: A Biblical Theology of Women in Ministry.* Downers Grove, IL: InterVarsity, 1995.

James, Carolyn Custis. *Half the Church: Recapturing God's Global Vision for Women.* Grand Rapids: Zondervan, 2011.

Spong, Martha, ed. *There's A Woman in the Pulpit: Christian Clergywomen Share Their Hard Days, Holy Moments & the Healing Power of Humor.* Christian Journeys. Woodstock, VT: SkyLight Paths, 2015.

## Discussion Questions

1. What experiences have you had with gatekeeping?

2. What makes referring to a female clergyperson as a pastor different from referring to a the same clergyperson as a lady pastor?

3. Why do you think hospitals are such common places for public acts of gatekeeping?

4. What role can or should the bishop or bishop's office have in "gatekeeping" the role of pastor in the church?

# 5

# When the Sanctuary Isn't

W hen the first women were ordained in 1970 in the ELCA's predecessor bodies the Violence against Women Act (1994) had not yet been conceived. And in 1970 there was not a single shelter for victims of domestic violence in the United States. Not one. The first shelter—Women's Advocates Inc.—opened in October of 1974 in Saint Paul, Minnesota.[1] By the late 1990s studies showed that though shelters were now in every state, there were still twice as many animal shelters in the US than there were shelters for women and children who were fleeing domestic violence. (The ratio is 3,800 to 1,500.)[2] And though the current number of shelters is difficult to ascertain, estimates are near two thousand— still far short of what is needed in a country where on average three women are killed by a domestic partner *every day*.[3]

In 1970 there was legally no such thing as marital rape. That is, every state had a legal exception in rape cases if the parties were married to each other. It was not until 1993 that these exceptions were abolished, with North Carolina being the final state to do so. Distinctions in the legal definition of rape based on the relationship between the victim and the perpetrator, however, still exist in some states—including South Carolina, which requires the use of

---

1. See Saint Martha's Hall, "History."

2. Office of the Clark County Prosecuting Attorney, "Fast Facts on Domestic Violence."

3. National Domestic Violence Hotline, comp., "Get the Facts & Figures."

a weapon or "violence, the threat of violence, or excessive physical force" in order to count as spousal sexual battery.[4]

Men are sometimes victims of interpersonal violence (including domestic violence and sexual assault) as well. An estimated twelve million people in the US experience some form of interpersonal violence every year. But there is a significant difference between what men experience and what women experience—in terms of both the frequency and severity of violence. Fifteen percent of all women in the US have received substantive physical injuries as a result of domestic violence, sexual assault, or rape compared to 4 percent of men. And 1 in 5 women as compared to 1 in 71 men have been forcibly raped.[5]

The problem with statistics is that it is easy to discount numbers. But behind each of these numbers is a real person, real people. People with faces; people with stories. And these stories do not remain outside the doors of the church. Neither does being *in* the church (as a member or as a pastor) decrease the statistical likelihood of domestic violence or sexual assault. In fact, some studies suggest that membership in a religious community may, in fact, exacerbate the problem. One study found that the average length of marriage for religious victims of domestic violence was 11.4 years compared to 8.6 years for nonreligious victims. In the case of religious victims, the abuse had continued for an average of 9.4 years, whereas for nonreligious victims the figure was 7.4 years. Religiosity of the victims bore no relationship to the severity of the abuse—so church attendance has no bearing on the level of violence endured—but it does seem to lengthen the number of years a woman is willing (feels required?) to endure it.[6]

In a 2014 study cosponsored by LifeWay Research and Sojourners in which Protestant senior pastors were asked about domestic violence, less than a quarter of the pastors said they believed domestic violence was occurring within their own congregation

---

4. See Wikipedia, s.v. "Marital Rape." See also Law Office of James R. Snell, Jr., "Understanding."

5. National Domestic Violence Hotline, comp., "Get the Facts & Figures."

6. Horton et al., "Women Who Ended Abuse," 235–46.

whereas nearly 75 percent of the pastors named it as a major problem within their broader community. Perhaps for this reason, 42 percent of all of the pastors acknowledged having *never* mentioned domestic violence within the context of any sermon or public talk, and an additional 22 percent said they may mention it once a year.[7] That is, two-thirds of Protestant pastors surveyed acknowledge that *at most* they might mention domestic violence once in any given year. And it is interesting to note that this study seems to assume that the pastor (who is probably male) is the one helping a victim (who is most likely female). It does not consider the possibility that the pastor may also be a perpetrator or a victim.

## Domestic Violence

In my interviews I never once asked a question about domestic violence. And yet in more than 10 percent of my interviews with female pastors, in response to the question, "What makes ministry hard for you?" personal stories of experience with domestic violence were shared. As high as this may seem, it is statistically low when compared to the general public. According to the National Coalition against Domestic Violence, nationwide 1 in 3 women have been physically assaulted by an intimate partner.[8] Each of the women who shared stories of domestic violence with me either is or was divorced. This is also not statistically normal, as many women in a violent marriage never leave. And for those who do, it takes—on average—seven attempts to leave before the relationship is finally successfully dissolved.[9]

For one pastor, the violence began before she went to seminary. She was working in the church as a lay volunteer when she was

7. LifeWay Research et al., *Pastors.*

8. National Coalition against Domestic Violence, comp., "Statistics"; National Domestic Violence Hotline, comp., "Get the Facts & Figures."

9. This statistic is well known in domestic violence awareness and prevention circles and is commonly referenced on websites devoted to supporting survivors of domestic violence. See for example Martin, "How to Stay Away for Good."

encouraged by her synodical bishop to consider a call to full-time ministry. When she talked with her husband about this his only response was, "You can go to seminary as long as it doesn't change my life." So, she says, "I took care of the house, and of my husband, and of my children. I did everything I had always done and more trying to make sure my school wasn't interfering in our home life. *And* I was a student." But, it was impossible to do everything perfectly and right, which led to an escalation of violence at home.

She said in her first call she served a church that was using its parsonage as a domestic violence shelter, and that working with and in the shelter became a central part of her ministry. However, "it also made me realize that I was living with domestic violence. And I could not continue living this way. These women helped me find my way out of an untenable situation." She credits the women she was helping with saving her life as they gave her the courage to leave the relationship.

Her bishop, however, was less helpful. He told her that if she were to divorce her husband, she would be removed from the roster. She remembers feeling torn at this point: she knew she could not stay in her marriage, and she knew, just as certainly, that she was called to stay in the ministry. The bishop finally relented, and she was allowed to remain on the roster but "*I* was required to do a psych eval and seek counseling. It felt like I was being blamed for my abuse all over again, but now by my bishop and by the church." Though her bishop's threat to have her removed from the roster was not a credible threat (divorce is not cause for such action), she did not at the time know this.

Another pastor I interviewed who shared a very little bit about of her story of domestic violence (she was clearly uncomfortable talking about it and did not share many details) said that she had been part of a clergy couple and that her husband was verbally abusive from the beginning of their marriage, but that she did not then see the abuse for what it was. She believed that she was not being a good enough wife. Though they both served as pastors, she did all of the housework and simply could not keep up. What began as emotional violence gradually became physical, and when her husband became violent with their small child, she knew she had to leave. She also went to her bishop for counsel before initiating a divorce. She remembers her bishop being very kind and sympathetic, but "though he knew that our divorce was, in part, because of domestic violence he let my husband stay where he was (so as not to hurt his ministry) and told me I needed to take a call in another part of the synod."

Being engaged in the ministry may enable women to find the help and support they need and leave a violent marriage. This was the case for several of the women in my study. However, it again bears mentioning that the only women who shared stories of domestic violence with me were divorced from their abusive spouses. If statistics are to be believed (and most experts suggest that domestic violence is greatly *under*reported), a significant percentage of female clergy may continue to live in situations of violence.

In addition to experiencing domestic violence as adults, several pastors shared stories of having grown up in violent homes. For at least one of the women the abusive parent was a father who was a pastor. Another woman said that her abusive, alcoholic father was part of what drew her more deeply into the church: "I was always at church. I loved church because it was safe. I wasn't safe at home. But at church I was safe." And one pastor noted that her abusive childhood with an unpredictable and explosive father gave her an advantage: "I was used to standing still and just waiting for the storms of an alcoholic father to blow over. When there are problems in the church, I know I can stand still and wait for this storm to blow over too." Many male pastors have also grown up in abusive homes, but the gender and power dynamics that may continue to play themselves out in a congregational setting leave women particularly vulnerable. When a woman who has grown up learning to stand still and wait out the storms finds herself in the midst of conflict with congregation members—especially if they are male and aggressive—she may find herself in an emotionally unsafe place.

## Intimidation and the Threat of Violence

Given the statistics on violence against women, it is inevitable that there are female clergy who have experienced interpersonal violence not only in the home but in the community as well. One pastor shared an absolutely harrowing story. When she was eighteen years old, she was stabbed multiple times in the face. She survived but was left blind in one eye. She left the church at the time, unable to reconcile what had happened to her with her notions of a loving God. But, she says, "I was only able to stay away for about a year. I knew I was missing something. So I came back and I prayed that God would use my suffering to help others who had suffered." Years later, after seminary, her bishop sent her paperwork to a congregation who did not want to interview her because the community "is too dangerous for a woman." The bishop told them to talk to her and she was called there. "They didn't know me. They didn't know how much I had been through and how much I could help others who were scared and hurting. It ended out being a great call."

Threats of violence are present not only in the community; they also arise within the walls of the church itself. One pastor shared a story of being in the office when a large, intoxicated man came into the church demanding food. The pastor said she and the female church secretary were alone. "I had no food to give him— we didn't keep any—but I gave him directions to the food pantry." He was insistent. She was to give him something immediately. She repeated that she couldn't, and "he hovered over me, held his fist back and threatened to hit me. Because I didn't know what to do and I knew I couldn't stop him anyway I told him to go ahead. I think he didn't know what to do so he left." She says that it is hard to believe retrospectively that she was that calm. "And of course we locked the door and I immediately fell apart when he left."

And, unfortunately, sometimes the threats of violence can come from within the congregation itself. One pastor tells of having been cornered in the sacristy after a congregational meeting by a man who was yelling at her and gesturing wildly. When she refused to engage, telling him they could talk when he calmed down enough to talk rather than scream, he yelled that she didn't understand or care about the congregation. It was not until members of the congregational council came into the sacristy to see what was going on that the man stopped the verbal assault. Another pastor likewise told of an older male member of the congregation yelling at her in public, following her around the fellowship hall, and then "telling me that I need to join him in the storage closet so that we could have this conversation in private! Of course I said hell no!" And, when she told her male colleague about this incident, his only response was to nod his head and say, "Yes, that's just how he is."

One pastor shared a story with me about another female pastor friend of hers who was at the time of my interview being stalked by a member of the congregation. Her congregational council had been unhelpful. They had blamed her for inviting "those people" to the church. (She has been doing ministry in an underprivileged and underserved community surrounding the church building while the congregation remains mostly white and middle- and upper-middle class). When she has reached out to her bishop and bishop's office for help, she has been told she needs better boundaries, that she needs not to be too "nice" to "people like that." And when she has reached out to law enforcement for help with an order of protection, she has been told it cannot be served because the man is homeless and unemployed, so there is nowhere to serve them.

Another, similar story was told by a pastor who serves a parish in rural Appalachia that has not received women in ministry well. Soon after she accepted the call to this congregation, she learned that the only other female pastor in town had received death threats when she was first ordained. And she describes the congregation she is serving as having a number of bullies, many of whom make it clear that they consider her something they have settled for only because they are small and rural and unable to afford a male pastor. During one Saturday morning church cleanup, she said she had to leave before they were done cleaning. "I was leaving for church business. But as I said goodbye to one couple at the door, the man approached me, finger-wagging, literally hitting me on the nose, and hissed, 'How *dare* you leave us here before the church is clean!' This would have never happened to a male pastor," she mused, "Aside from the finger-wagging and literally standing over me, looking down, clearly chastising me like a child, he would never have expected a male pastor to clean the church in the first place." As we talked about this incident, she said that she later realized the man's behavior constituted assault, but the couple has since left the church because the man didn't "believe in women pastors."

The same pastor described an incident with another male bully in the congregation who she described as very physically aggressive, and who was yelling at her about hymn selection one Sunday. "He literally followed me around the church. I tried to politely end the conversation, invited him to the worship committee meetings when hymns are selected. And then excused myself and went into the bathroom. He stood outside the bathroom door and continued yelling at me. His behavior was extreme enough that other members of the congregation now stand with me after worship if he is there." And yet another man, a council member, sits and glares at her during meetings. "He cracks his knuckles if he doesn't like what I'm saying. He knows what he is doing. He is trying to intimidate me. And it works. I don't really think he will hurt me, but he clearly wants me to remember that he could."

When I asked one woman what her greatest challenges in ministry were, she said that one of the biggest difficulties is older men "who are not used to women in authority. They try to bring you down a notch, whether it is conscious or unconscious." I asked if she could offer an example. "He is a very large man. And I am not a small woman, but he will use his size. Whenever he disagrees with me or wants me to do something he will stand right over me, trying to intimidate me. And then he'll say things like, 'I've got a granddaughter who is older than you.' to minimize whatever I am saying." One time he said some very demeaning things about LGBT folks in Sunday school and she called him on it. She said this behavior escalated after that. She said she finally felt that she had to say something about his behavior to the church council. Male council members responded by being more present when he was around. "I don't think they went far enough, but at least they tried to do something."

Of the eighty-five women I interviewed for this book, five reported having experienced physical altercations of intimidation that stopped short of physical violence, four reported having had to seek help from council members and other church leaders to deal with physical threats and intimidation from parishioners, and an additional four have had to ask for orders of protection to be placed on parishioners or others affiliated with the congregation who posed a continual threat of physical violence, sexual violence, or both. When I asked her what she wanted me to do with this information, one of the women responded: "I don't really know. But it would help if my male colleagues, if my male bishop, at least knew this stuff."

## Sexual Harassment

The social media #MeToo movement went viral in the fall of 2017. The purpose of the movement is to bring attention to the prevalence of sexual violence and sexual harassment around the world. The #MeToo movement was a powerful enough force in 2017 to be named *Time* magazine's Person of the Year. One of the things #MeToo made clear was that whereas an estimated 25 percent of all women have been sexually assaulted or raped, sexual harassment is a common experience for the vast majority of women and girls, if not for all.

Perhaps unsurprisingly, most female clergy have experienced varying levels of sexual harassment. It ranges from hearing demeaning language related to their vocation ("pastorette," "lady pastor") to enduring catcalls and comments about their bodies to to facing more overt intimidation and unwanted physical contact. I was recently speaking with a group of about twenty female pastors. I asked how many of them had experienced sexual harassment *in ministry*, and at least half of them raised their hands. Here are a few—but by no means all—examples women shared with me. Many women mentioned parishioners (and others) commenting on their appearance—their bodies—in inappropriate ways. One woman shared that after she had lost a significant amount of weight, an older male parishioner patted her on the backside and said, "Well now, you're looking good." Another woman had an older male parishioner follow her around the fellowship hall during a public event, insisting, "Pastor, give me kiss! Come on, lay one on me." She said she had to confront him—tell him to stop. "It was creepy. For several weeks my husband stood with me in the line after worship so that guy would know he was there." Another was told, "But, Pastor, I *need* a kiss. For comfort." And another pastor said, "There is a creepy old man in the congregation where I serve now who has asked me if I pole dance. Who the hell asks that?! I try to avoid being near him. I really don't know how to handle things like that. It's just creepy." Another woman was told by a male parishioner that her sermons would be easier to listen to if her alb were wet.

Most of the women take experiences like this in stride. It did not begin when they became clergy, but it did morph. One woman commented: "Most of the problems are fairly minor. But they are consistent, and you can just get flat worn out. But it could be worse, no one's thrown stones or spit on me. I know folks that has happened to." And several women concluded stories of harassment with comments like, "But I haven't been assaulted. Many of my parishioners or friends or colleagues haven't been as lucky." This sense that it could have been worse—and that therefore worse could happen in the future—is a common feeling. Another pastor told me, "After one funeral, while I was riding back to the church from the graveside—and it was forty-five-minute drive—I was hit on by the funeral director. It was icky and weird. It never reached the level of scary, but still . . ." and her voice trailed off, not finishing the sentence but speaking volumes in the silence.

Another pastor told of having received a phone call from a family member of a man who was a very infrequent member of the congregation. He was an alcoholic with serious drug- and alcohol-related health problems and he had been, again, admitted to the local hospital. The family member told the pastor that the man wanted a pastoral visit, "though in retrospect," she said, "I'm not sure it was the man himself who wanted me to visit and not the family member wanting me to 'save' him." The visit itself was fairly routine. She said they talked a few minutes. But though he was polite enough, it was clear he did not really want to talk. So she said a prayer and told him he would be in her prayers and that he could call if he wanted to talk more later. Well, later he did call. But he began the conversation with, "What are you wearing?"

> I know I should have ended the conversation immediately, but it caught me off guard. So, I think I said something like, "I'm sorry. Excuse me?" So he repeated the question. And while I was too stunned to respond he followed this with more inappropriate questions that rather quickly became rather graphic in nature. As I realized what was happening I ended the conversation, telling him this was inappropriate, and I hung up the phone. But this continued to happen. He called me on my cell phone and he called me on my office phone. Both the intensity of the calls and their frequency increased. So, I spoke with the council chair about it. He agreed I needed to no longer visit this particular parishioner. That only further escalated his calls. I ended out telling the whole council about it one evening and they decided to contact the police and have a restraining order taken out. I was really, really grateful for the support of the council—I knew they had my back. But I also felt very conflicted about the situation. I couldn't help but wonder what I could have or should have done differently. I hate feeling like I gave up on someone.

And that sense of feeling bad about having given up on someone was expressed by every single pastor who had to refuse contact with a parishioner, even when they know it was what they had to do for their own safety.

As disorienting as such events are for many pastors, several reported that the incidents of sexual harassment that most haunt them have come from their colleagues. And at times the harassment, assault, or both, began in seminary. One pastor described what might be called serial harassment and assault. She said she was repeatedly harassed by one male classmate over a period of months. The harassment ranged from inappropriate text messages to obscene comments in private to aggressive public behavior during which the male student made clear his disdain for the ordination of women. The pastor then said that one night on campus, at a community event, after imbibing in a significant amount of alcohol, her male colleague cornered her near the bathroom—in a space that though public was somewhat secluded—and put his hand up her dress. She said that she reported this to the appropriate seminary authorities and was told that he came from a long line of pastors.

This same pastor shared that she knows she is not the only seminarian to have had such experiences. In fact, she says, one of her female friends dropped out of seminary after being raped by a classmate. Unfortunately, such experiences are not limited to seminary or graduate school. Quite a few pastors noted that they had overheard male colleagues discussing their bodies in clergy gatherings (cluster or conference meetings, for example), and a number of pastors told stories of disrobing after a synodical event as the only female clergyperson (or as one of only two or three) when male colleagues whistled or catcalled as they took their albs off. In each case the female pastor was quick to tell me that "they didn't mean any harm," or, "I know it was just a joke." But each pastor remembers feeling very uncomfortable, and none of the pastors who told of such experiences remembers anyone willing to speak up—in one instance, a bishop included—and address the inappropriateness of the behavior. Everyone in the room nervously laughed it off. The bishop, she noted, did not participate in the whistling; but neither did he put a stop to it. The sense that others would laugh it off, and especially that her bishop—the one person in the room with the power to make the greatest change in the atmosphere—would laugh nervously as well rather than stand up for them left many of the woman not only feeling unsure of themselves but—as one woman said—"it also made me aware of how vulnerable I was. Even, and maybe especially, with my colleagues."

Some experiences of sexual harassment from colleagues go far beyond anything like attempts at humor to direct threats. One pastor remembers, "I was leading a Boundary Training session for our synod when a retired pastor, known for being abrasive and obstinate, stood up, looked at me and said, 'You should know that if I want to have sex with you, I will.'" The female pastor said she does not recall what, if anything, she said in reply. What she does remember is that no one else spoke up. "It was as if nothing ever happened."[10]

## Pastoral Care

For many women, their own experiences with domestic violence, sexual assault, or harassment due to their gender has made them very intentional allies for other vulnerable people. This is manifest publicly in advocacy work, in preaching, and in pastoral care. Quite a few of the clergy I interviewed recognized that their gender opened conversational doors that may not have been as easily opened for men. And several further noted that their own experiences gave them the empathy to hear parishioners into speech regarding their own experiences of violence and harassment.

Quite a few women told stories of women who had come to them for pastoral care related to previous—or in some cases on-going—instances of domestic violence or rape. One woman spoke hesitantly to one of the pastors interviewed about violence against women in a very generic way. The pastor followed up. Though it took months of follow-up conversation, the pastor learned that the female parishioner had told the previous male pastor that she was

10. Every three years all rostered leaders in the ELCA (pastors and deacons) are required to participate in Boundary Training workshops that address power and authority particularly in the parish. The provision and oversight of Boundary Training is the responsibility of individual synods. Anecdotally it seems that most synodical Boundary Training is focused on the sexual and financial responsibility of parish leaders as persons of power and authority within the congregational setting.

being abused and he had told her to "go work it out." (It should be noted that this is a recent occurrence—a story from the twenty-first century, not from the 1970s.) The female pastor assured her it was not in her power to "work it out" and it was not God's will for her to live in such a situation. And the pastor helped the woman out of her marriage. Once she was on her own and doing well, she told the pastor, "God sent you here for me."

Another pastor tells of having a middle-aged woman who came to her for help in coming to terms with childhood incest. "She had tried to talk with the senior pastor before I was called here. But he simply doesn't have the same emotional IQ and she left his office feeling worse rather than better." Once she began speaking with the new female associate pastor, and at the encouragement of that pastor, the woman began counseling and has, in the words of the pastor, "been born again. It has been beautiful to watch."

Most such stories are similarly of private pastoral care moments. But a handful of the female clergy shared stories of the ways in which their own experiences of gendered violence and harassment coupled with the realities of the world led to some very public opportunities to speak out against violence. One pastor remembers that the week after the Stanford rape case,[11] the story of Bathsheba was the lectionary reading. So, in her sermon she preached, "it's a bad week for women." She addressed women's voices not being heard in the text, historically by the church, and in our current society. Four people—each an older white man—walked out during the sermon. She was disconcerted when it happened but determined to continue. When she tried to talk with the men afterwards, one told her, "I don't think we need special interests groups and I'm tired of having this stuff shoved down my throat." But she also shared that she had more women whisper words of thanks as they were leaving church that day than on any day before or since. And several of these women followed up in the next week or so to share their stories. One woman told her, "It's been twenty years. But it still hurts. It never goes away. I never talk about it because no one heard me then.

11. Koren, "Telling the Story."

Today is the first time I've felt like the church cared about people like me." The pastor then told me that though it hurt to know that she had angered and alienated some of her parishioners, "Being able to speak a word of grace and hope to these women is far more important than the discomfort caused to people who chose to be oblivious to white, male privilege."

Several women also expressed the ways their own experiences of marginalization have shaped the way they interpreted scriptures and preached, particularly in regard to other marginalized communities. As one pastor said regarding the continuing tension over the ELCA's decision to ordain and marry members of the LGBTQ community: "I have to be an ally. Twenty years ago the cherry pickers tried to keep me from following God's calling on my life. Me being an ally now comes square out of me being a female clergy and having others who have been—and are—allies for me." This is not at all to suggest that straight white men cannot be allies. Of course they can. As one woman said, "We need all of our male colleagues to speak up as allies because they still have more power." But for many women a sense of duty to advocate on behalf of others is grounded in their gratitude for those who had advocated for them.

Female pastors do not, however, just care for women, children, and marginalized communities. They provide pastoral care for everyone in their community. One woman told me that she knew several of the men in her congregation had not wanted her to be called as pastor because she was a woman. Knowing this, she said, "gave me the opportunity to learn how to love those who did not love me." And she did. At least one of these men is now one of her biggest supporters.

Several of the female pastors commented that they have found their gender sometimes to be a gift in pastoral care of male parishioners. "My gender opens doors for some men, too, I think. They feel less compelled to project a macho image when their lives are in a mess than they might with a male pastor." Another pastor said that she thinks pastoral care is easier for her because she is freer (socially) to ask about emotions. When she visits patients in the hospital, she often asks family members to leave. And then she will asks the patient—especially when they are close to death—what they are afraid of. "I have had some of the most amazing holy ground moments at times like these." She goes on to say, "Of course, my male colleagues may do the same thing, but I do sometimes think people let their guard down more quickly with me."

## A Peaceable Kingdom?

The text revision of *The Diagnostic and Statistical Manual of Mental Disorders* (*DSM-IV-TR*), published in 2000, defined a traumatic event as occurring when "both of the following were present: (1) the person experienced, witnessed, or was confronted with an event or events that involved actual or threatened death or serious injury or a threat to the physical integrity of self or others [and] (2) the person's response involved intense fear, hopelessness or horror."[12] Trauma, in other words, is determined by an individual's emotive response to an event rather than by the event itself. In *DSM-III* trauma had been defined as "an overwhelming event that was *outside the range of usual human experience.*"[13] In other words, it was the abnormal nature of the event itself that largely determined whether or not something could be considered trauma. The language was changed primarily in recognition that much of what has been considered trauma (and has required the ongoing psychiatric care determinative of trauma) is, in fact, empirically within the range of ordinary human experience for a statistically significant portion of the population. In short, the medical profession now recognizes the statistical "normalcy" of trauma.

The church, likewise, needs to recognize its frequency while continuing to name the violence that is behind such trauma as sin. The church has got to stop pretending that domestic violence and sexual assault don't happen in our congregations; they do. We have pastors who perpetrate violence, and we have pastors who

12. Quoted in Miller, ed., *Interventions for Addiction*, 188.
13. Quoted in Jones and Cureton, "Trauma Redefined" (italics added).

are victims of violence. We need to be addressing both. As I said at the beginning of this chapter, every pastor I interviewed who spoke of domestic violence was divorced and spoke of it as a past-tense event. The reality, however, is not so simple. These pastors were serving in congregations while being abused; other women continue to serve in congregations while experiencing domestic violence at home. It is important to note that the only women who spoke to me about their own personal experiences with domestic violence where doing so in order to address questions of their relationship with their bishops. And it is equally important to note that for each of these women the reason they spoke to their bishop about domestic violence was *not* because of the violence but because they had initiated divorce proceedings and knew this was not something they could hide. Domestic violence itself, on the other hand, remains largely hidden.

Because the women who spoke to me of domestic violence all spoke of their interactions with bishops who are either retired or are serving in a synod outside of the purview of this study, and because none of them described a process that was experienced as life-giving, I sent all of the bishops in the study area some follow-up questions. I asked them if any of the rostered leaders in their synods had brought experiences of domestic violence to them, and I asked if they had a plan for how they would respond if and when this did happen, particularly if the abusive partner was also a rostered leader.[14]

The response of the bishops was twofold: a pastoral response to the victim of violence and a disciplinary one for the offender (assuming the offender is also a rostered leader). Each of the bishops who responded said their primary concern would be pastoral care for victims—including providing counseling, encouraging

14. None of the bishops I spoke with had had any of the rostered leaders in their synod share stories of living with domestic violence. One bishop had helped one of the pastors in his synod help the pastor's child leave a violent marriage, and one bishop had—as a senior pastor—helped one of his colleagues. And one bishop shared that he currently has a rostered leader who he has reason to suspect of domestic violence, but that when he has reached out to the rostered leader's spouse, she has denied any abuse has occurred.

victims to report to authorities, helping victims acquire any necessary restraining orders, and meeting their immediate needs for safety. One of the bishops said that if the offender were a rostered leader, then the bishop would turn to the ELCA's document *Vision and Expectations* and argue that the call to trustworthiness in one's relationships (both in the church *and* in the home) would offer sufficient grounds for pursuing the removal of an offender from the roster in the case of domestic violence. Another one of the bishops said that if the offender were also a rostered leader, the bishop would "possibly pursue a disciplinary hearing/removal from the roster. The ELCA constitution (20.21.01) states that 'Ordained ministers shall be subject to discipline for . . . conduct incompatible with the character of the ministerial office.' Domestic violence, in my mind, is clearly such an incompatibility." Another bishop likewise leaned on the constitution, saying, "I think there is enough leeway in the constitution to remove someone for domestic violence. It is something I would absolutely be willing to go through an ecclesial trial for."

It is the "in my mind" and "I think" part of their responses that stuck out to me. So, I pushed back a bit with each of the bishops about the removal from the roster of someone guilty of domestic violence. I asked—for the sake of clarification—"Is removal from the roster in a case of domestic violence at the discretion of the bishop? Is this a matter of interpretation?" In short, all of the bishops said yes it is. The ELCA has no clear policy to remove someone from the roster for domestic violence, even if that violence includes child abuse. So, I asked a bit more: Do we not have a clear policy that removes someone from the roster in situations of sexual misconduct, even when said misconduct is between consenting adults? This response came from one of the bishops: "We are encouraged to 'zero tolerance' for sexual misconduct, harassment, etc., and, as I said, domestic violence clearly fits that category to me, but perhaps it should be made clearer." Another bishop said that the zero tolerance for sexual misconduct was, at least to a large extent, a matter of legal protection for the church.

"There is, unfortunately, less legal pressure to protect spouses from violence in the home."

The bishops I spoke with were very helpful. Several expressed profound sadness when I shared with them that the divorced pastors who had shared stories of domestic violence had not felt they could go to their bishops for help. One noted, "I did not become a bishop to be a bureaucrat. But that is what the church has turned this office into. It is tragic to me to think that someone would not feel safe going to their bishop if they are suffering from domestic violence." The bishops clearly want the church to be more proactive. But it seems to me the wiggle room allowed to the bishops for addressing perpetrators of domestic violence but not for sexual misconduct is a symptom not merely of institutional lethargy but of a culture hyperconcerned with the policing of sexual behavior and simultaneously hypersaturated with—and tolerant of—violence. As one of the bishops said, "We have not come to a point as a culture to say that domestic violence is unacceptable. That makes it harder to draw clear lines in the church." Add to this an ambivalence about gender roles that is still evident in the church, and it comes as hardly a surprise that we are, as an institution, doing little to prevent domestic violence, and doing even less to adequately address it when we cannot not see it.[15] Neither the current ELCA constitution nor the current *Vision and Expectations* document (a document that details expectation for all pastors and deacons serving the church), however, addresses domestic violence. As I have been writing this book, the ELCA has been in the process of revising *Vision and Expectations*, so I asked Greg Villalon, the ELCA's director for missional leadership and candidacy, if the current draft of the revised document addressed domestic violence.

15. Additionally, when I shared an early draft of this chapter with one young woman, her immediate response was, "But what if the bishops," who are usually male, "are perpetrators? Then what?" Hers is a great point. The church needs to seek accountability regarding both sexual misconduct and domestic violence at *all* levels. The current *Vision and Expectations* document, which details the expectations for behavior (including sexuality) of all rostered ELCA leaders, does not address domestic violence. This seems like a necessary, though hardly sufficient, place to begin.

He graciously responded that it did not, but he thanked me for raising the question and said he "would make sure the drafting team included it."[16]

Perhaps for the same cultural reasons mentioned above, when women shared stories of intimidation and threats of violence they experienced in the parish, the common thread between them was shame. Female pastors are hesitant to share these stories with their bishops—especially with male bishops—because they are afraid such experiences reflect badly on *themselves* rather than on the persons perpetrating the violence. Women who have not experienced support in ministry because of their gender are afraid that acknowledging such realities as intimidation and threats simply gives ammunition to those who argue that women are not strong enough (physically or emotionally) to be in such public leadership roles. And many of the women expressed having believed at the time that on some level they somehow or other "deserved" such mistreatment for not being good enough.

One bishop noted, "I think we're learning. Part of the gift of female leadership—when it was a boys' club, it was about taking care of one another. Women in ministry open this up." The unique struggles of women in ministry call into question some of the previous assumptions about power and privilege. Another one of the bishops, who is all too aware of such experiences of violence, told me, "Telling the stories is powerful. We don't hear these stories. We hear about a glass ceiling, but we miss the individual stories of pain and woundedness. But because we miss the stories of woundedness, we also miss the opportunities for profound healing." Theologically, it is critical that we hold that God does *not* cause such situations of suffering. God does, however, work through them. Because more women (relative to men) have experienced the trauma of violence, they have a particular gift to offer a church which is also populated by those who have experienced the trauma of violence.

16. This conversation took place as an email exchange on January 15, 2019, and is shared with Pastor Villalon's permission.

## *Suggested Resources*

Evangelical Lutheran Church in America. *Vision and Expectations: Ordained Ministers in the Evangelical Lutheran Church in America*. Rev. ed. Chicago: Evangelical Lutheran Church in America, 2010. http://download.elca. org/ELCA%20Resource%20Repository/Vision_and_Expectations_for_ Ordained_Ministers.pdf/.

LifeWay Research, et al. *Pastors and Domestic and Sexual Violence*. Cosponsored by LifeWay Research, Sojourners, and IMA World Health, July 2014. Conducted between May 7 and May 31, 2014. http://lifewayresearch. com/wp-content/uploads/2014/07/Pastors-and-Domestic-and-Sexual-Violence.pdf/.

Fortune, Marie. *Love Does No Harm: Sexual Ethics for the Rest of Us*. New York: Continuum, 1998.

Heath, Elaine A. *We Were the Least of These: Reading the Bible with Survivors of Sexual Abuse*. Grand Rapids: Brazos, 2011.

Herman, Judith Lewis. *Trauma and Recovery: The Aftermath of Violence—from Domestic Abuse to Political Terror*. Rev. ed. New York: Basic Books, 1997.

## *Discussion Questions*

1. What resources about domestic violence awareness, prevention, and healing do you know of in your community? Is domestic violence discussed in your church community? Why or why not?

2. Were you surprised by the violence reported by female pastors? Why or why not?

3. Most of the pastors expressed being very unsure how to know when to report inappropriate behavior. How do you know when behavior has transitioned from undesirable to harassment?

4. What policy related to sexual violence and domestic violence do you think the church should have?

5. Read Isa 11:1-9. What would the peaceable kingdom look like for women in our churches and homes?

# 6

# Changing the Narrative

Alice laughed: "There's no use trying,"
she said; "one can't believe impossible things."

. . .

"I daresay you haven't had much practice," said the Queen.

"When I was younger, I always did it for half an hour a day.

Why, sometimes I've believed as many as six impossible
things before breakfast."

—ALICE IN WONDERLAND

Theologian and pastor Sam Wells suggests that sin is often a lack of imagination. We fail to be faithful because we are unable—or unwilling—to imagine life as God intends. The faithful development and use of our imagination allows us to see the world as it could or should be—and in an important eschatological sense the way it *really* is—rather than the way it appears to be because of the way it has been. A healthy imagination can make the seemingly impossible not only possible but probable.

But the human imagination is not limitless. We cannot imagine something for which we have absolutely no frame of reference. If I give a stick to a young child, the child's imagination may seem limitless: the stick can be a baseball bat or a weapon or a horse or a tent post or . . . But whatever the stick becomes for the child, it does so because the child already has some image of a bat or a weapon or a horse or a tent post or . . . The child's imagination appears boundless to the adults in the child's world, but it is in fact limited by the child's real-world experiences.

This is true of adults—and of communities—as well. Individuals and congregations who are unable to receive the gifts of women in ministry leadership positions are often simply unable to imagine that such a thing is possible. And sometimes because folks may be unable to imagine female clergy, they are assumed to be imaginary, in the category of unicorns. As one pastor said, "Once a woman asked me what I did. When I told her I was a pastor, she stared at me in disbelief and said, 'I've heard of women pastors, but I've never actually *seen* one!'" The pastor said this interaction left her feeling like a zoo exhibit.

Many pastors shared similar stories. Most of the pastors I interviewed reported regularly hearing that they were the first female pastor someone has ever seen, heard, or met. And quite a few of the pastors themselves said that it was not until they first met a female pastor that they began to imagine the possibility for themselves. "Even though I grew up Lutheran and even though most of my life the Lutheran Church has been ordaining women, I was an adult, a public school teacher, before I ever heard a woman preach. It created a cognitive dissonance for me as I had never imagined a female pastor. But once I had seen one I could no longer ignore my own call to the ministry."

This cognitive dissonance is often what opens us to imagine something new or different. Lois Lowry's book *The Giver* is a dystopian young adult fantasy novel set in a community that has lost its ability to see color. Twelve-year-old Jonas is talking to a friend who is tossing an apple in the air and catching in. Though he does not know what it is, because he has no language for it, Jonas suddenly sees the color red as the apple flies through the air. Once he has seen color—and learns that it *is*—he can never again unsee it. This causes a cognitive dissonance that goes far beyond an inability to return to a life of monochromatic gray; it begins a ripple that changes his entire world.

For many women, the cognitive dissonance associated with experiencing a woman in ministry can be a very powerful, life-changing hermeneutical shift. One pastor told me a story of a time when she was leading a women's retreat. During the closing worship service at the end of the retreat, one of the participants began weeping. The pastor asked her about it after the service. "She told me that she saw the elements on the table during worship and realized that she had been waiting on a man to come in and serve the Eucharist. And then she realized a woman could do it and she was overcome." Many of the pastors shared their own similar experiences. "Knowing that something is possible for someone *like* me makes it a thinkable thought *for* me." Such experiences create a cosmic shift. For women who have felt called by God into public ministry but who had no experiential framework, or even language, for what they have felt, receiving communion from a female pastor has often been the experience that has made the unimaginable thinkable.

This experience is not unique to Lutherans. A recent study (rather unsurprisingly) found that girls and young women who have female clergy role models are considerably more likely to consider the possibility that they too might be called into the public ministry.[1] And more than that, the study also found that women (regardless of their own sense of vocation) who had female clergy role models reported significantly higher levels of self-esteem than those who had never had a female clergy role model. But the difference women role models make as pastors or priests affects not only how churchgoers view their clergy. The same study found that the way worshipers conceptualize God may be directly connected to formative experiences with clergy and gender: "We found evidence that people's view of God as either authoritative or gracious is dependent on the gender of their religious leaders when young. This is important because those who tend to view God as more gracious than authoritative also have increased levels of well-being, happiness, and self-esteem, all of which are integrally important for personal empowerment."[2]

---

1. Knoll and Bolin, *She Preached the Word*, especially chapter 7.

2. Knoll and Bolin, *She Preached the Word*, 143.

The same study found that even if a particular individual has no experience with a female pastor, a denominational gender-inclusive leadership policy increases "religiosity, spirituality, and especially congregational efficacy/identity among women and sometimes even among men."[3] Women *and* men are positively influenced by the reality that both men and women are needed in and called to church leadership. Having visible female pastors changes everything. It makes a new reality possible because it becomes a thinkable thought.

Most, if not all, of the women I interviewed commented on the importance of female ministry role models: "I've always been very blessed with great bishops and clergy colleagues. Having a strong and pastoral woman who serves as assistant to the bishop has been a tremendous blessing for the women in this synod. I don't think we can overestimate the power and importance of that sort of public role model."

And male colleagues also recognize this important role. One pastor who did her internship in a church with a multipastor staff as the first woman said that when she left, the senior pastor told her, "Thank you for giving my daughter an example of a woman as a pastor. Something I could never do for her." And several bishops and assistants to bishops noted the importance of women in visible synodical roles. "Seeing women serve in more visible roles has given many of the women in our synod the courage to imagine themselves doing it." The bishops are all quick to note how vital a role female leaders play in their synods, and all commented on their gratitude for the spiritual and pastoral leadership the women in their synods provided, not just in their own congregations, but on a synodwide level. And two of the (male) bishops also commented that there were female pastors in their synods whom they would love to have as their own pastor.

The pastors I interviewed are acutely aware of the importance of their visibility to and mentorship of younger women and girls. One pastor said, "When I wear my stole I am never not aware that I wear it not just for me but for all the women who are called to this

3. Knoll and Bolin, *She Preached the Word*, 190.

but will never be allowed to do so and for the countless women who have been silenced in the past." The weight of the responsibility of being a voice for the voiceless is immense. But so, nearly every pastor I spoke with confirmed, is the sense of honor and privilege and grace.

To receive such grace and to recognize the honor and privilege in the midst of the complexities and responsibilities women bear in parish ministry requires a robust theological imagination. And, imagination requires courage because imagination subverts the status quo. Once we imagine the world in a new and different—and arguably more faithful—way, there is not going back. Several years ago I was teaching a course on immigration. My students read a book that detailed the political and cultural practices that forced migrants to cross the US-Mexico border through the most dangerous part of the desert while at the same time making it illegal to provide water stops along the way (by charging anyone who left water for those making the trek with littering). One of my students rather angrily asked me "What the hell am I supposed to do now?" When I asked him what he meant, his response was, "I can never again not know this. So, now I have to *do* something about it." This student's ability to imagine the plight of those attempting to immigrate into the United States led to a cognitive dissonance that he knew would change his life permanently.

## Status and Stasis

As of spring 2018, when a historic six new female bishops (including the first two African American female bishops and a Latina bishop) were elected, the ELCA's Conference of Bishops now has fifteen female bishops out of a total of sixty-five bishops. This is in addition to Bishop Elizabeth Eaton, our denomination's first female presiding bishop. During the election cycle social media was abuzz with excitement over the shifting demographics within the church.[4] Not everyone was happy, however. As I scanned

4. See, for example, Miller, "'She Is Loose.'"

comments on various websites, I also found a less significant but nonetheless consistent thread of comments that exhibited a combination of concern and anger because, in short, "Women will take over the church." Other more triumphal and less anxious but equally ill-founded comments suggested, "Finally, woman have achieved equality in the church."

Both the concern that women will take over and the claim that equality is a reality seem a bit dubious based on the actual numbers. If the presiding bishop is not included, the Conference of Bishops is now 23 percent female. If the presiding bishop is included the Conference of Bishops is now 24 percent female. This hardly suggests gender parity or the loss of status for men in the church. However, if sociologists are correct—or even just correct-ish—the ELCA has, indeed, reached a tipping point that suggests that change, though slow, will continue.[5] There is, in other words, no going back. Thanks be to God. As one of the bishops told me, "Female leadership is part of who we are as ELCA. If you are ELCA that means women are leaders." And of course the shifting demographics of public leadership does not exist solely in the church, because the church does not exist in a cultural vacuum. Women are blazing paths across the spectrum. Women in leadership is a political reality. That is, women in positions of public ministry are a real—and enduring—part of public life.

A number of the older women I interviewed—those in ministry twenty-five-plus years—expressed having felt like early on in their ministry things seemed to be improving rapidly for women. And then they reached a plateau. The situation did not (necessarily) get worse, but it seemed to stall. The sexuality wars of the early part of this century (especially the ELCA's 2009 decisions on

5. The idea of a "tipping point" was made popular by Morton Grodzins in the 1960s to explain "white flight," the point in time when white families would begin moving out of a predominantly white neighborhood as it integrated. Tipping points can be a negative, as in the case of "white flight" or a good, as in the case of racial diversity and gender inclusion.

Sociologists suggest that when 10% of a given population firmly accept a new practice or belief, that practice will, in time, be adopted by the entire population.

same-gendered relationships) seemed, to many women, to create a backlash that they found surprising. "It seemed like people who had come to terms with female pastors but could and would not come to terms with gay pastors now wanted to turn the clock back forty years." Congregations (especially in geographic areas where a female pastor already made them "too liberal" in their social context) panicked when their denomination's leadership made a decision based on what some congregation members saw as based on political correctness (which they could dismiss) rather than based on justice (to which ELCA leaders were called and to which member faith communities might be called). These congregations are now much more likely to be vocal in refusing a female pastor than they would have been fifteen years ago. A bishop told me of one such congregation that began the process of leaving the ELCA because of the ELCA's naming of patriarchy in the 2018 "Draft Social Statement on Women and Justice."[6] "Patriarchy," he was told, "may have existed a hundred years ago. But not today." This refusal to hear women's stories of their own experiences of patriarchy leads to a "resistance to women in ministry that is much more subtle today than it was when I started in ministry nearly thirty years ago. It is more subtle and less prevalent. But still present. And still just as insidious." And this resistance comes from both men and women.

Change is inevitable; the opposite of change is death. But change is slow and sometimes painful. The situation for women in ministry (and in public leadership more broadly) is the experience of retrograde motion. That is, there is clear movement forward. And yet as soon as that forward movement is perceived as a threat institutionally or communally there is a backlash that seems to stall progress or even cause a (momentary) regression. But this backlash is temporary and is and will be followed by even greater momentum forward. Women—as Nicholas Kristoff and Sheryl WuDunn remind us—hold up half the sky.[7] Women make up more than half of most worshiping communities. Women will

6. This draft statement has now been published by the Evangelical Lutheran Church in America, as *Faith, Sexism, and Justice*.

7. Kristof and WuDunn, *Half the Sky*.

continue to grow in leadership in the church. I do not think this is a question. But *how* it will happen and what the church can do to faithfully facilitate this change is a critical question. It is a question of discipleship, part of discerning what it means to be the body of Christ (to borrow from Presiding Bishop Eaton) together and for the sake of the world.

## Now What?

As I worked on this project, I began to doubt the wisdom of having undertaken it. On the one hand, it has been great fun. I have met and become friends with some amazing female leaders in the ELCA. I have also met become friends with our bishops, and I developed a tremendous amount of respect and gratitude for them and for the gift they are to us. Yet, on the other hand, I have received some very difficult stories, stories that shine light on the brokenness of the church. As I have wrestled with how to tell the stories I've heard faithfully and unflinchingly—especially the stories in which the church is responsible for sin, complicit in sin, or both—I have been reminded of Luther's explanation of the second use of the law—to act as a mirror and show us our sins when its first use (to curb sin) has failed. More importantly, we are called to look into the mirror of the law so that we can see more accurately where we are, not so that we can feel bad about our sin (though that may be a good and necessary response), but so that we can adjust our common and individual lives in such a way as to be more faithful, more pleasing to God. And this is, of course, the third use of the law.

What follows are the three areas—broadly construed—where the church has the most work to do: boundary training, equitable employment practices, and faithful hermeneutics and catechesis. I have separated them for heuristic purposes, but in practice they are of a piece; movement forward in one area is linked to movement forward in each area. And just beneath the surface of each of these, necessarily holding them up, is the critical role played by bishops and bishops' staffs. A church that faithfully lives into its mission must equip both men and women for both lay and ordained leadership. And a crucial component of equipping women for ordained leadership is the encouragement and support from each bishop and all of the synod leadership.

## Boundary Training

Several of the women I interviewed brought up Boundary Training. Both the content and implementation of Boundary Training appear to be quite uneven across the synods. As long as boundary training is and remains an item on a checklist that is reduced to "Don't have sex with parishioners and don't use church money for personal purchases," as one pastor summed up her experience, Boundary Training will have no positive impact on rostered leaders. Another pastor said that her most recent experience with Boundary Training "seemed unduly focused on the dangers of pornography. Especially on church computers." She felt alienated by this experience as not only did it not address the very real boundary issues she felt that she has as a female pastor, but she felt that it reflected "something intangible but disturbing about some of my male colleagues." Boundary Training should not, she went on to say, "feel" like a boundary violation. But it did.

A number of pastors commented on the failure of Boundary Training to address their most pressing needs. Most of the Boundary Training seems to assume a one-way power dynamic that has a male pastor and female parishioner as its model. For this reason, Boundary Training always assumes that the pastor is in a position of power; but this fails to take into account the complexities of power and gender relationships when the pastor is a female. Most Boundary Training also fails to take into account collegial relations even though for most of the female pastors interviewed, it is the failure of collegial boundaries that causes them the most distress. Most of the women I interviewed are the only female pastors in their conferences. Women who felt they had strong, supportive male colleagues felt much better equipped to address the gendered boundary issues that came up in the congregation. But women who feel unsafe emotionally—and in some cases physically—with their male colleagues rather predictably feel the most isolated and the least equipped to address issues within their congregations.

An additional reflection made by several female pastors is that the Boundary Training they have attended has failed to address the unique boundary challenges faced by female clergy. Among these challenges is the need to be more attentive to physical safety than are their male counterparts. One of the bishops I interviewed was very aware of this need. He noted that the female clergy in his synod were uncomfortable with late afternoon meetings in his office if it meant leaving the building after dark. Male clergy—including the bishop—had not considered the physical safety concerns of the environment surrounding the synod office. And even when male clergy are willing to address such concerns (this bishop, for example, takes the time to walk visitors back to their cars now), the mental and emotional energy that female clergy require for such mundane tasks is rarely recognized. This safety tax can be exhausting and expensive.

Closely related to the additional boundaries women require are comments many women made about the additional time they are expected (by their families, their congregations, the wider community, and themselves) to allot to caregiving—time their male colleagues are not expected to spend in the same way. Though a few of the female pastors did lift up that their spouses share fairly evenly in household and childcare responsibilities, most of the pastors expressed taking on much of the caregiving and emotional support work at home, and most of the pastors expressed feeling like the invest considerably more emotional energy in the lives of their staff than their male colleagues do. Women are encouraged to attend to self-care needs, but self-care is not possible without the ability to establish and maintain healthy boundaries. None of the women I interviewed—not a single one—expressed wishing that they invested less. But many of them expressed the recognition that while they are busy caretaking, some of their male colleagues who are not are, as one pastor said, "enabled by the system to be the synodical steeple-chasers."

Here is a final note about Boundary Training. Several of the female pastors commented that they know they have male colleagues who do not keep up their Boundary Training. In fact, several of them named male colleagues they have heard declare that they would not "waste their time" with the synodically mandated training. I asked several bishops about this and the majority of them acknowledged the problem but said that until and unless someone is looking to change calls they have very little power to enforce such a policy. One of the bishops, however, suggested more creative ways to ensure compliance. Moving forward if the church can find ways to broaden Boundary Training, then the church could be a leader and model in healthy professional relationships. (For instance, the female pastors' criticism suggests that much more that could be done to take into account the particular boundary challenges for not only female clergy but also clergy of color and LGBTQ+ clergy as well.)

## Equitable Employment Practices

Another significant quality of life issue for female pastors is financial. The gender pay gap is real and substantive. And synods can and should address this. Several bishops suggested, if anecdotally, that the pay gap for pastors with comparable levels of experience serving in congregations with similar congregational profiles may be as high as 20 percent. And both bishops and the assistants to the bishops that I spoke with acknowledged that within their synods the vast majority of the highest-paid pastors are men. The reverse is also true: the vast majority of the lowest-paid pastors are women. Several pastors commented that their male colleagues knew this *and* that some blame female pastors for lower salaries across the board: "As the ministry becomes seen as 'women's work,' all of us will be paid less." In addition to all of the emotive issues of self-esteem and the righteous anger at the injustice of pay inequity, the pay gap leaves women—especially those who are single—particularly vulnerable in regard to retirement.[8] As one divorced pas-

---

8. In 2018, equal pay day in the United States was April 10. This means that

tor told me, "I'll never retire. I simply won't be able to. I've always served small churches, and I've never been paid what I was worth. I feel bad saying that, but it's true. And so now I'm stuck. And the church isn't going to help me."

An additional financial stressor for many female pastors is maternity leave. Many churches suggest that women use sick leave when they have a child. And many women have been encouraged by their congregational councils or senior pastors to reduce their hours, to become part-time, when they have children. For some women, the ability to work reduced hours is a gift, but for many it is an additional financial burden, especially when they don't feel they have the freedom to make the decision that is best for them and their family. I was in a meeting with female church leaders in which maternity leave was being discussed. One woman suggested that paid maternity (or family!) leave policy should be a part of *all* call conversations: The ELCA teaches that sex is good, that women can be pastors, and that abortion is always a last resort. This means pastors will have babies." The church should be a social and cultural leader in conversations about employment and family leave. Still, we have a long, long way to go.

Directly connected to the financial insecurity of the church's female leaders is the lack of representative female leadership in the larger congregations of many synods and in synodical leadership positions such as conference dean. Women continue to have less of an impact across the church because they continue to experience what many have referred to as the "stained glass ceiling." Even in a church body like the ELCA, which honors women's gifts for ministry, women find themselves unable to move into larger leadership positions. When I asked several groups of women why this was, they expressed having received no direct leadership training ("I didn't get *that* in seminary!") and indeed having received clear but

---

women had to work until April 10 in 2018 to earn what their male counterparts earned in 2017. This is a national average; no data suggest that women in the church are doing any better than the national average. See WIkipedia, s.v. "Equal Pay Day" (https://en.wikipedia.org/wiki/Equal_Pay_Day/).

mixed social messages: "We want you to lead. But not too much. Lead like a girl. Whatever that means."

All of these factors lead to overextended, stressed female pastors, who often feel incredibly isolated and lonely. Many of our church's pastors are in need of pastoral care—care they do not feel they can safely ask for, and care they often do not think they deserve. Many of the pastors expressed carrying a deep sense of inadequacy and failure. Rather than experiencing their struggles in ministry as evidence of the sinful realities of patriarchy, they have internalized these realities as indicators of their own moral or character defects. The shame and fear that "I" might be the problem leads to even greater isolation from one's peers, further exacerbating the problem for many, many gifted leaders.

## Faithful Hermeneutics and Catechesis

I began this chapter with the cognitive dissonance that seeing women in ministry creates. This dissonance is caused by a contradiction between what one has been taught to believe as immutable truth and one's own experiences, whether these are experiences with a female pastor or of feeling called to ministry. Those who oppose women in ministry often express their reasons in pious language. That is, opposition to women in ministry is presented as an argument about scriptural authority. Usually "Paul says . . ." The not-so-subtle implication of such an argument is that to deny a particular reading of Scripture (one that subordinates women to men and prohibits women from public leadership roles, especially in the church) is to reject the authority of Scripture. Such a stance renders discussion void insofar as it rules any alternative hermeneutic unfaithful.

The cognitive dissonance that experience with a woman in ministry—the experience that something that can't be in fact is—is an opportunity for catechesis, a chance to learn about the complexities of biblical hermeneutics. For many people—women *and men*—this hermeneutical shift can validate an internal sense, a way of knowing, that the patriarchal practices of the church have more to do with outdated cultural norms and unfaithful attempts to maintain power than they do with a faithful interpretation of the gospel.

Though I do not mean to suggest that those who oppose women's ordination on the grounds of scriptural interpretation are all necessarily doing so as a way of maintaining the status quo in terms of ecclesial power—most, in fact, are no doubt struggling to be faithful—in practice that is exactly what they are doing. But overthrowing the status quo is something Jesus was pretty well known for. And even though many who oppose women's ordination do so trying to be faithful, insofar as they refuse to acknowledge the legitimacy of other possibilities, they turn scriptural hermeneutics into a weapon rather than a tool of discipleship. Faithful Scripture interpretation requires a willingness to wrestle with difficult texts—neither to dismiss them nor to assume that the status quo interpretation is nonnegotiable.

One of the pastors I interviewed was in the midst of telling me a story about her interactions with the Evangelical pastor of her childhood. She was recounting all the reasons he gave her that "proved" that she did not hear God calling her into the ministry. He told her that by continuing down the path she had begun (the very path that brought her into the ELCA), she was failing "to faithfully submit to God's will for her life as a woman and as a wife and a mother." She paused after she said this to me and then looked me in the eyes and said, "I. Call. Bullshit." We both laughed, of course, but upon later reflection I realized that this pastor is what Luther would call a theologian of the cross. A theology of the cross, Luther taught, is a theology that calls a thing what it is. It calls sin sin. The continued defense of a patriarchal system that subjugates women is the system that prohibits women from ordained leadership. Not Scripture. Not Paul. And certainly not Jesus.[9]

9. And not the ELCA. Churches often use "religious freedom" as an argument for gender discrimination. But the theology of the ELCA does not support this. That God calls men *and* women into public ministry is not up for debate within the ELCA; this question has been answered. Thus, our congregations should not be allowed to discriminate under the banner of "congregational autonomy" or "religious freedom."

I have neither the space nor the expertise to adequately address the exegetical and hermeneutical questions related to women in ministry, though I do offer some suggested resources on this topic at the end of this chapter for those who are interested or need additional theological and scriptural references. However, here are a few highlights. Women were the first witnesses of the resurrection (Matt 28:1–10; Mark 16:6–7; Luke 24:1–10), and Mary Magdalene was, by definition, the first apostle sent by Jesus to tell the story of the resurrection (John 20:16–18).

And even though much of the weight of the argument against women's ordination is found in the writings of Saint Paul, Paul himself lifts up a number of female leaders. Paul only uses the word *diakonos* for those who served the early church in a formal capacity—preaching and teaching. This is exactly the language Paul uses for Phoebe (Rom 16) and Euodia and Syntyche (Phil 4). New Testament scholar (and Pauline expert) Richard Hays says, "When Paul uses this language about struggling alongside him in the work of the Gospel, this is quasi-technical language for describing the work of preaching the apostolic message. He does not simply mean that they went along and made the coffee."[10] And lest one be inclined to read the exegesis of scholars like Hays and dismiss it as postmodern attempts at political correctness, bishop and theologian Saint John Chrysostom (in the fourth century) also believed that Euodia, Syntyche, and Phoebe were *diakonoi* in the church. Later ecclesial arguments over what it means to be a deacon and a priest notwithstanding, women have in fact served in ecclesial leadership roles from the time of Jesus. To continue to argue against such based on the witness of Scripture is dubious at best.

At Pentecost the Holy Spirit was poured out—was given—to all. To men and to women. Yet Paul's famous eschatological claim, "There is no longer Jew or Greek, there is no longer slave or free, there is no longer male and female; for all of you are one in Christ Jesus." (Gal 3:28) is only experienced now to the extent that we, the church, fully embrace the gifts of all for ministry, regardless of

10. Hays, *New Testament Ethics*, 70.

gender.[11] This is an integral part of the gospel the church has been called to teach and to preach but as a means of living as grateful and grace-filled witnesses of Jesus' love for all.

## Suggested Resources

Bessey, Sara. *Jesus Feminist: An Invitation to Revisit the Bible's View of Women.* New York: Howard/Simon & Schuster, 2013.

Hays, Richard B. *New Testament Ethics: The Story Retold.* J. J. Thiessen Lecture Series. 1998. Reprint, Eugene, OR: Wipf & Stock, 2018.

Knoll, Benjamin R., and Cammie Jo Bolin, *She Preached the Word: Women's Ordination in Modern America.* New York: Oxford University Press, 2018.

Kristof, Nicholas D., and Sheryl WuDunn. *Half the Sky: Turning Oppression into Opportunity for Women Worldwide.* New York: Random House, 2009.

Streufert, Mary J., ed. *Transformative Lutheran Theologies: Feminist, Womanist, and Mujerista Perspectives.* Minneapolis: Fortress, 2010.

## Discussion Questions

1. How important have role models been in your own life?

2. Change can be very hard. How do we overcome our resistance to change for the sake of the gospel?

3. What is the role of male allies in working for gender equality in the church (and elsewhere)?

4. How has your inherited framework for Scripture interpretation shaped your own reception of women in ministry?

5. What do you hope for the church in ten years? Twenty-five? Fifty?

---

11. And, for that matter, regardless of sexual orientation or identity.

# Acknowledgments

G iven the struggles of pastoral ministry for women, it is worth asking why they do it. When I asked the female pastors this question, their answers were unanimous variations on a theme: It's all about grace. Quite a few of the woman responded that their own experiences of God's grace and of having received it in church, particularly at the altar made them want, more than anything else, to share this grace with others. "I just know that I receive God's grace and it matters. It matters in ways big and small. In ways I can't even begin to express. But it matters to me and it matters to others." Because their own lives had been irrevocably changed for the better, these pastors continue to yearn to be instruments of that grace. Presiding over the Eucharist was—as one might imagine— by far the most commonly mentioned aspect of pastoral ministry that both brought women into the ministry and continues to keep them there. "I love presiding at the table. It is an honor. A blessing. It is one of the places where I know God shows up." And, as long as God continues to show up, they do too.

The second most common answer to the question of why do this is a sense of being called to proclaim the Gospel. "I love preaching. I have a word. People count on me to help them see what difference being a Christian makes." Nearly two dozen of the women interviewed shared experiences of having heard the Gospel "as if for the first time" as a significant part of their call story. For many women this desire to share the gift of grace they have received through proclamation of the Word drives them. "There are so many false gospels. So many false gods. And all of them enslave. It is such an honor to help people discover the freedom of God's love and grace. And I get to do this every week."

Working on this project has been an amazing experience; one in which I, too, have been able to say "Wow. I get to do this every week!" Every writer is, I imagine, acutely aware of how little of their work they could have done on their own. This is particularly true of this text. I am profoundly grateful for the amazing women—busy women who are about the work of ministry and who are about the work of ministry in a world that does not always welcome them—who invited me into their lives and shared their stories with me. The warmth and grace, the humor and honesty they embody has made me a better scholar and, I hope, a better person and more faithful follower of Christ.

I am also grateful to all of the bishops I interviewed as well as their staffs. No human institution is perfect and the ELCA is no exception. However, my work with the ELCA's bishops has helped me to fall in love with my church. This is especially true of my own bishop, Bishop Tim Smith. Working with Bishop Smith and the staff of the NC synod (Pastor Danielle DeNise, Pastor Sara Ilderton, Deacon Tammy Jones West, Catherine Fink, and Pastor Phil Tonnesen) continues to be life-giving in ways I could not have anticipated. And the opportunity to interview our Presiding Bishop, Bishop Elizabeth Eaton was not only interesting, but just plain fun. Each of these people shaped this book both directly and indirectly. And I am grateful to call each of them friend.

The NC Synod has embraced the work of—in Pastor Danielle DeNise's words—changing the landscape of ministry for woman in powerful and far-reaching ways. One result of the work of the NC Synod Bishop's staff has been a larger conversation throughout Region 9 of the ELCA (the synods of Virginia, North Carolina, South Carolina, South-Eastern, Florida-Bahamas, and Puerto Rica and the Virgin Islands) that has led to a regional relational agreement signed by all of the bishops that commits to very concrete steps to continue the work of justice and equity for women in the church. It has been a joy and a privilege to work with, in addition to Bishop Smith, Bishops Humphrey (VA), Yoos (SC), Gordy (SE), Suarez (FL-Bahamas), and Negron (PR-VI) as well as with Deacon Connie Schmucker (FL-Bahamas), Pastor Ginny Aebischer (SC), and Dr. Mary Streufert who serves as the Director for Justice for Women. The women and men engaged in this important work have provided me and this project with love and support that exceeds anything I might have ever imagined asking for.

I am also deeply grateful to work at Lenoir-Rhyne University. I have amazing colleagues and students. I want to thank three colleagues in particular, Drs. Beth Wright, Veronica McComb, and Paul Custer. The four of us worked together in a writing group throughout the time I was completing the final edits on this projects. Their feedback made this a better book. I am also grateful to my colleagues in the Religion program—Drs. David Ratke and Jonathan Schwiebert. For the past seven years their collegiality, support, and friendship have made coming to work a joy. Other colleagues who have supported me in this project in many various ways throughout the past three years include Drs. Devon Fisher, Michael Deckard, Jennifer Heller, Amy Hedrick, Julie Voss, Taylor Newton, and Mrs. Debbie Tonnesen. I am, in fact, surrounded by wonderful colleagues for whom I am grateful, including our University Provost, Dr. Gary Johnson who approved my sabbatical as I was completing this work.

This project could not have happened without a generous grant from the Louisville Institute. Their Project Grant for Researchers funded the travel that allowed me to conduct nearly one hundred interviews. Louisville's commitment to the church and to public theology is a gift that is far greater than any single project they support.

And I am grateful to the staff at Wipf & Stock. They have demystified the process of taking a book from idea to text. And everyone I have worked with has offered me grace and kindness. From the earliest conversations with K.C. Hanson, through to the final typesetting work of Calvin Jaffarian and to James Stock and his work with marketing, working with Wipf & Stock has been a joy. And special thanks to Jeremy Funk for his careful attention to detail and his push for theological clarity. The book is better because of his work. Though, of course, any deficits remain my own.

And last but not least—because the last are truly first—I am profoundly grateful to and for my family. They feed me literally and figuratively. My husband, Russell, has been an unfailing source of grace and support for me. My children, Hannah and Jordan, became real adults during the time I was working on this project; watching them become the adults they are has been a source of tremendous joy, as well as humility. They have all responded to my fits of isolation and absent-mindedness with remarkable humor and kindness. They care about both me and the work I am doing. They have all (along with Jordan's fiancé, Sam) read various drafts of the manuscript, asked questions, and, at times, argued with me. And through it all they have loved me. Russell, Hannah, Jordan, and Sam, thank you! I love you more than words can say.

# Appendix

7/17/16

Miss [REDACTED]

I saw you on TV and noticed you had a collar around your neck. Are you a Bishop or a member of the clergy?

Have you read 1st Timothy, chapter 3, verses 1-5? (King James of course.) I don't believe you qualify for any office of the clergy.

I am concerned about your soul. Let me ask you this question. Do you know Jesus? I don't mean in your head, but in the heart. There is a vad difference.

Have you ever realized you are a sinner? Romans 3:23 "For all have sinned, and come short of the glory of God."

Have you ever ask Jesus to forgive you of your sins? Romans 6:23: "For the wages of sin is death: but the gift of God is eternal life through Jesus Christ our Lord."

Last, but not last! Romans 10:13: "For whosoever shall call upon the name of the Lord shall be saved."

I pray you here don't this. No one has to go to hell, no one!

I have enclosed a gospel tract for you to read. Please do so.

Sincerely: Someone who is concerned about your soul!

# Bibliography

American Psychiatric Association. *Diagnostic and Statistical Manual of Mental Disorders: DSM-IV-TR*. Prepared by the Task Force on *DSM-IV* and other committees and work groups of the American Psychiatric Association. 4th ed. Washington, DC: American Psychiatric Association, 2000.

Bessey, Sara. *Jesus Feminist: An Invitation to Revisit the Bible's View of Women*. New York: Howard/Simon & Schuster, 2013.

Daly, Mary. *Beyond God the Father: Toward a Philosophy of Liberation*. Boston: Beacon, 1973.

DeConick, April D. *Holy Misogyny: Why the Sex and Gender Conflicts in the Early Church Still Matter*. New York: Continuum, 2011.

Evangelical Lutheran Church in America. *Faith, Sexism, and Justice: A Lutheran Call to Action*. Chicago: Evangelical Lutheran Church in America, 2019.

———. *Vision and Expectations: Ordained Ministers in the Evangelical Lutheran Church in America*. Rev. ed. Chicago: Evangelical Lutheran Church in America, 2010. http://download.elca.org/ELCA%20Resource%20Repository/Vision_and_Expectations_for_Ordained_Ministers.pdf/.

Evangelical Lutheran Church in America, North Carolina Synod. *Seriously? A Video of Actual Things Said to Women Pastors by Parishioners and Male Pastors*. Published October 10, 2018. https://www.youtube.com/watch?v=bTcaAkG86QQ&t=163s/.

———. "*Seriously?* Group Discussion Guide." Published October 2018. https://nclutheran.org/wp-content/uploads/2018/10/Seriously-Discussion-Guide.pdf/.

———. *Seriously?* Podcast series. 8 episodes. http://nclutheransynod.libsyn.com/.

Fey, Tina. *Bossypants*. 2011. Reprint, New York: Reagan Arthur, 2014.

Fiedler, Maureen E., ed. *Breaking through the Stained Glass Ceiling: Women Religious Leaders in Their Own Words*. New York: Seabury, 2010.

Fortune, Marie. *Love Does no Harm: Sexual Ethics for the Rest of Us*. New York: Continuum, 1998.

Gillam, Terry, and Terry Jones, dirs. *Monty Python and the Holy Grail.* Released 1975. Written by Graham Chapman et al. Starring Graham Chapman et al. Produced by Monty Python Pictures in association with Michael White Productions and the National Film Trustee Company. DVD. Hilversum, The Netherlands: Sony Pictures Home Entrainment, 2018. Also available on Netflix.

Grenz, Stanley, with Denise Muir Kjesbo. *Women in the Church: A Biblical Theology of Women in Ministry.* Downers Grove, IL: InterVarsity, 1995.

Guarino, Cassandra M., and Victor M. H. Bordon. "Faculty Service Loads and Gender: Are Women Taking Care of the Academic Family?" *Research in Higher Education* 58 (2017) 672–94.

Hays, Richard B. *New Testament Ethics: The Story Retold.* J. J. Thiessen Lecture Series. 1998. Reprint, Eugene, OR: Wipf & Stock, 2018.

Heath, Elaine A. *We Were the Least of These: Reading the Bible with Survivors of Sexual Abuse.* Grand Rapids: Brazos, 2011.

Herman, Judith Lewis. *Trauma and Recovery: The Aftermath of Violence—from Domestic Abuse to Political Terror.* Rev. ed. New York: Basic Books, 1997.

Horton, Anne L., et al. "Women Who Ended Abuse: What Religious Leaders and Religion Did for These Victims." In *Abuse and Religion: When Praying Isn't Enough,* edited by Anne L. Horton and Judith A. Williamson, 235–46. Lexington, MA: Lexington, 1988.

James, Carolyn Custis. *Half the Church: Recapturing God's Global Vision for Women.* Grand Rapids: Zondervan, 2011.

Jones, Laura K., and Jenny L. Cureton. "Trauma Redefined in the *DSM-5*: Rationale and Implications for Counseling Practice." *Professional Coun-selor.* http://tpcjournal.nbcc.org/trauma-redefined-in-the-dsm-5-rationale-and-implications-for-counseling-practice.

Knoll, Benjamin R., and Cammie Jo Bolin. *She Preached the Word: Women's Ordination in Modern America.* New York: Oxford University Press, 2018.

Koren, Marina. "Telling the Story of the Stanford Rape Case." *Atlantic,* June 6, 2016. https://www.theatlantic.com/news/archive/2016/06/stanford-sexual-assault-letters/485837.

Kristof, Nicholas D., and Sheryl WuDunn. *Half the Sky: Turning Oppression into Opportunity for Women Worldwide.* New York: Random House, 2009.

Lamott, Anne. *Almost Everything: Notes on Hope.* New York: Riverhead, 2018.

Law Office of James R. Snell, Jr. "Understanding Spousal Sexual Battery." Law Office of James R. Snell, Jr. (website). https://www.cdvlawyer.com/domestic-violence/felony-domestic-violence/south-carolina-spousal-sexual-battery/.

Leach, Tara Beth. *Emboldened: A Vision for Empowering Women in Ministry.* Downers Grove, IL: InterVarsity, 2017.

Lewis, Karoline M. *She: Five Keys to Unlock the Power of Women in Ministry.* Nashville: Abingdon, 2016.

LifeWay Research, et al. *Pastors and Domestic and Sexual Violence.* Cosponsored by LifeWay Research, Sojourners, and IMA World Health, July 2014.

Conducted between May 7 and May 31, 2014. http://lifewayresearch. com/wp-content/uploads/2014/07/Pastors-and-Domestic-and-Sexual-Violence.pdf/.

[MacArthur, John, et al.] *The Statement on Social Justice and the Gospel.* Drafted in Dallas, TX, in 2018. https://statementonsocialjustice.com/.

Makant, Mindy, interviewer. Interview with Presiding Bishop Elizabeth Eaton, February 23, 2017, Chicago, IL.

Martin, Sydney. "How to Stay Away for Good." Posted by Brian Nguyen under the title "Eliminate That Seven Times Statistic." In Survivor Spot (blog) on Break the Silence about Domestic Violence: BTSADV; the National Voice of Domestic Violence (website). January 15, 2017. https://www. breakthesilencedv.org/category/survivor-spot/.

Manne, Kate. *Down Girl: The Logic of Misogyny.* New York: Oxford University Press, 2018.

Miller, Emily McFarlan. "'She Is Loose': A Historic Group of Female Lutheran Bishops on #MeToo and the Holy Spirit." Instituions—News. Religion News Service, July 25, 2018. https://religionnews.com/2018/07/25/new-elca-female-synod-bishops-talk-metoo-religious-left-what-lutheran-looks-like/.

Miller, Peter, ed. in chief. *Interventions for Addiction.* Comprehensive Addictive Behaviors and Disorders 3. Amsterdam: Academic/Elsevir, 2013.

National Coalition against Domestic Violence, comp. "Statistics." National Coalition against Domesitc Violence (website). https://ncadv.org/statistics/.

National Domestic Violence Hotline, comp. Statistics. "Get the Facts & Figures." National Domestic Violence Hotline (website). https://www.thehotline. org/resources/statistics/.

Office of the Clark County[, Indiana,] Prosecuting Attorney, comp. "Fast Facts on Domestic Violence." Domestic Violence. Prosecuting Attorney, Clark County, Indiana; Fourth Judicial Circuit (website). http://www. clarkprosecutor.org/html/domviol/facts.htm/.

Piper, John. "Can a Woman Preach if Elders Affirm It?" February 16, 2015 (episode 533). In *Ask Pastor John* (podcast with transcript), MP3 audio. https://www.desiringgod.org/interviews/can-a-woman-preach-if-elders-affirm-it/.

———. "Is There a Place for Female Professors at a Seminary?" January 22, 2018 (episode 1151). In *Ask Pastor John* (podcast with transcript). MP3 audio. https://www.desiringgod.org/interviews/is-there-a-place-for-female-professors-at-seminary/.

———. "Should Women Be Police Officers?" August 13, 2015 (episode 661). In *Ask Pastor John* (podcast with transcript). MP3 audio. https://www. desiringgod.org/interviews/should-women-be-police-officers/.

Ramsey, Dave. "Marriage and Money—Dave Ramsey Rant." *The Dave Ramsey Show* (YouTube channel). August 11, 2015. https://www.youtube.com/ watch?v=q-vlioPLwKE/.

Saint Martha's Hall. "History of the Battered Women's Movement." Saint Martha's Hall: Breaking the Cycle of Domestic Violence (website). http://saintmarthas.org/resources/history-of-battered-womens-movement/.

Sandberg, Sheryl. *Lean In: Women, Work, and the Will to Lead.* New York: Knopf, 2013.

Spong, Martha, ed. *There's a Woman in the Pulpit: Christian Clergywomen Share Their Hard Days, Holy Moments & the Healing Power of Humor.* Christian Journeys. Woodstock, VT: SkyLight Paths, 2015.

Streufert, Mary J., ed. *Transformative Lutheran Theologies: Feminist, Womanist, and Mujerista Perspectives.* Minneapolis: Fortress, 2010.

Thompsett, Fredrica Harris, ed. *Looking Forward, Looking Backward: Forty Years of Women's Ordination.* New York: Morehouse, 2014.

Unkrich, Lee, and Adrian Molina, dirs. *Coco.* Starring Anthony Gonzalez et al. Written by Lee Unkrich et al. Produced by Darla K. Anderson et al. Produced by Walt Disney Pictures and Pixar Animation Studios. 1 DVD. United States: Disney, 2018.

Wikipedia. "Marital Rape in the United States." https://en.wikipedia.org/wiki/Marital_rape_in_the_United_States#cite_note-ncvc.org-4%20/.

Wolf, Naomi. *The Beauty Myth: How Images of Beauty Are Used against Women.* New York: HarperCollins, 2002.

Woodard, Colin. *American Nations: A History of the Eleven Rival Regional Cultures of North America.* New York: Penguin, 2011.

Made in the USA
Columbia, SC
14 November 2019